AF449771

Giuseppe Salvago Raggi

The Only Man
Dressing for Dinner

Italian Ambassador Giuseppe Salvago Raggi
at the Siege of the Legations

Gingko Edizioni
2019

The Only Man Dressing for Dinner
Italian Ambassador Giuseppe Salvago Raggi
at the Siege of the Legations

ENGLISH translation: Angelo Paratico

Copyright © 2019 Gingko Edizioni
Vicoletto Valle n° 2, 37122 - Verona (VR)
www.gingkoedizioni.it

ISBN 978-88-31229-03-6

First edition: September 2019

Graphic project: Ploy Web Studio

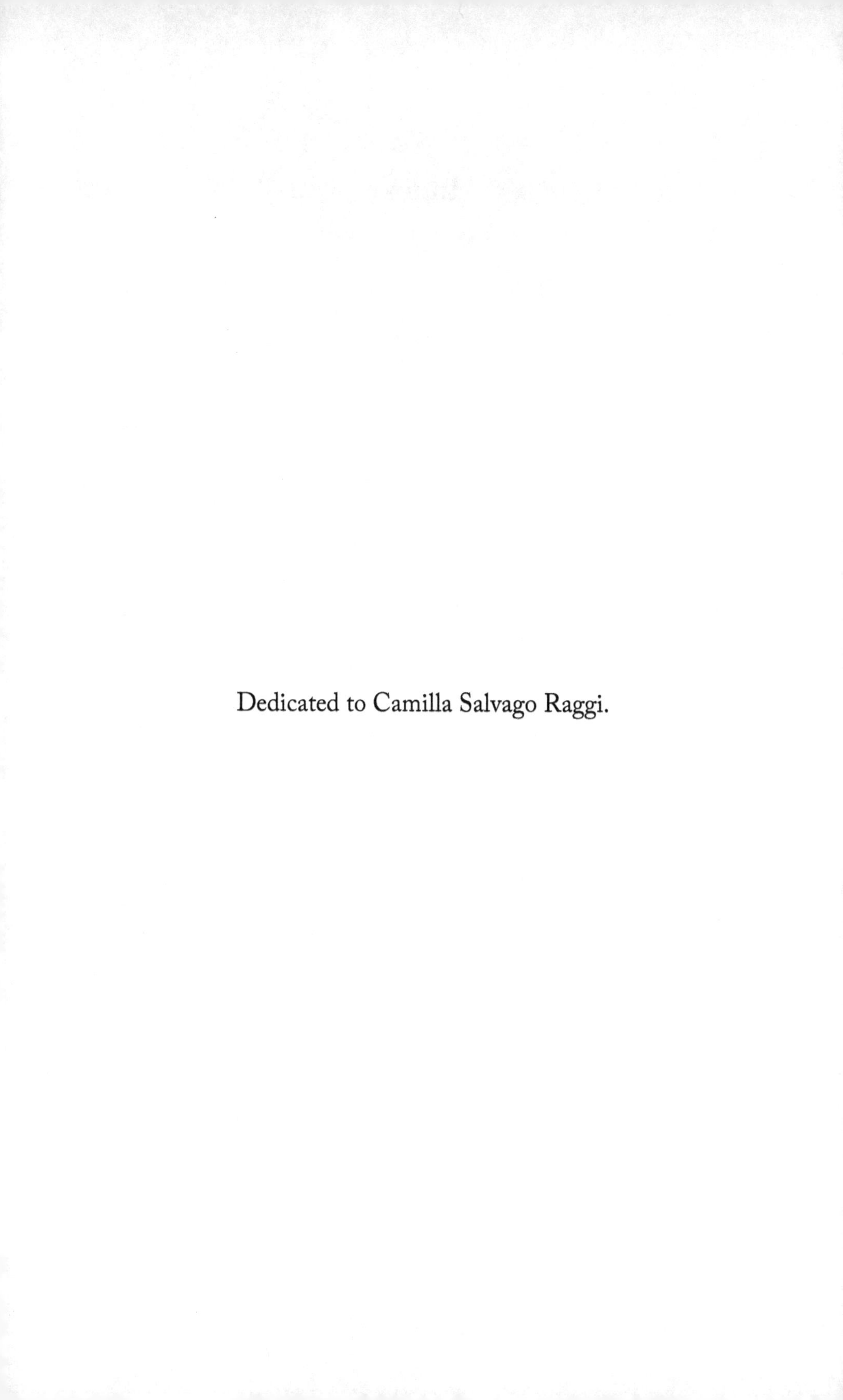

Dedicated to Camilla Salvago Raggi.

Index

Nobody thinks of dressing for dinner, except the Marquis Salvago, and I think it shows things are truly far gone when English people dine, but do not dress.

Polly Condit Smith

Giuseppe Salvago Raggi at 18

Introduction

Giuseppe Salvago Raggi, known to friends and relatives as Pippo, was born on 17 May 1866 in Genoa, into an ancient family. The Salvago family appears in the *Cronica* written by Giovanni Villani[1] as one of the most powerful within the Genoese Republic. Paris Salvago, Pippo's father, was a member of the Italian Parliament and founder of the magazine *Annali Cattolici* later transformed into *Rivista Universale*.

Violantina Raggi, his mother, was a descendent of Tommaso Fieschi Raggi, sent to London by King Philip II of Spain as his Ambassador to the Court of Queen Elizabeth I. She died soon after his birth and he was sent to a school in Florence: this, combined with the economical use of words typical of the Genoese, may explain the beauty of his prose.

After his university degree, in 1889, he was convinced by his father to apply for a diplomatic career but failed the exam because it was rigged, and another candidate was placed in front of him. Giuseppe's father went to complain directly to the Prime Minister, Francesco Crispi who, unsurprisingly, took no action: as a young man, he had similarly flouted the rules. Giuseppe embarked on a long voyage to forget the injustice suffered, visiting Egypt, Jerusalem and Istanbul. The collection of his quaint letters he wrote to his father was published in 1972 under the title of *Lettere dall'Oriente*. During that trip, he had the privilege, for a few days, of travelling with the discoverer of Troy, Heinrich Schliemann and, once back in Italy, he gave another try to diplomacy and that time he was accepted. Soon after he was dispatched to Madrid, the next posting was Saint Petersburg and, in 1891,

---

1. Giovanni Villani (1276-1348).

Berlin. On 19 October 1891, he married Camilla Pallavicino and, on the 7 December 1892, Paris, their son, was born.

In March 1894 Salvago Raggi was in Cairo, assisting Minister Alberto Pansa, working in close contact with the British representative, Lord Cromer. From that strategic position, he could witness the folly that would lead Italy into the 1896 bloody disaster of Adowa.

In 1897, he was dispatched to Beijing where he remained - except for a short interruption - in charge of Italy's Legation until 1901, finally returning to Italy through Mongolia. Then, from 1902 until 1914, he was posted to Africa, first to Cairo, then as Governor of Eritrea. In 1915, when Italy entered WWI, he dutifully enrolled as a simple artillery officer, despite being 49 years old. He had been an advocate of Italy's neutrality, but since the King had decided to enter the fray on the side of Great Britain and France, he ceased his opposition to the conflict. In 1915 his estranged wife, Camilla, who had been with him through the Siege in Beijing, died in Milan and, soon after, Pippo took a new wife, Giuseppina Menotti.

At the front, he fought valiantly for one year, being promoted to captain of Artillery but then, because of his expertise in diplomacy and administration, he was summoned to Rome and sent to Cairo.

Immediately after the war he was posted to Paris as Ambassador and, together with Vittorio Emanuele Orlando[2] and Sydney Sonnino[3] he was a member of the Italian delegation discussing the terms of peace with Germany and Austria at Versailles. By April 1919, sensing all the flaws contained in that treaty, which the victors wanted to force on the losers and forecasting with clarity which the final consequences would be, he felt compelled to resign.

---

2. Vittorio Emanuele Orlando (1860-1952). Italian Prime Minister at Versailles in 1919.

3. Sidney Costantino Sonnino (1847-1922). Italy's Foreign Affairs Minister in 1919.

Camilla Salvago Raggi Pallavicino

Salandra thought him stupid, while the more measured Sonnino told him that he was an egoist and his true motive was to avoid trouble.

Salvago Raggi pointed out in his memoirs that: "In reality the Versailles Treaty had the appearance of being very hard on Germany, as Clemenceau wanted it to be, but it had been drawn up in a way that offered to the vanquished nation an escape route to avoid almost all of the harshest conditions imposed upon her… This was the real flaw of the Treaty and the responsibility fell mainly on Great Britain, which favored the reconstruction of Germany's power, without thinking that the Germans, monarchists or republicans or democrats or socialists or Hitlerians, would set out to accomplish the program contained in a commemorative plaque they had placed in 1922 at the University of Berlin in memory of the students who had fallen during the war: *Invictis victi victari.*"[4]

During the twenty years of Fascist rule, Giuseppe Salvago Raggi seldom travelled to Rome, even though he had been nominated Senator, favoring a sort of self-imposed exile. He kept on looking with dismay at all the political developments, noticing the false steps and the weakness of Italy, while writing comments and critical articles, which are still for the most part unpublished.

He wrote his memoirs in the early thirties, sitting in the shadow of a nut tree, at his villa of Campale. In the last pages, he presented a vivid encounter with the young Benito Mussolini in October 1922, a few hours after being appointed Prime Minister of Italy by the King. What the 39-year-old Mussolini wanted from the old diplomat was a briefing about the Versailles Treaty and the Spa Conference. Salvago Raggi spoke to him for hours over a period of two days and, despite being impressed by Mussolini's quick grasp of those complex situations, he did not hesitate to talk bluntly to the young man, comparing him to the *sorcerer's apprentice* who knew how to make water spring from the ground but not know how to stop it, and came out of that meeting convinced that: "… with one like him the last man talking is right."

He died on 28 February 1946, shortly before the referendum which sent his beloved King into exile and inaugurated the Italian Republic.

Only one chapter of Salvago Raggi's memoirs is presented here. Specifically, the one related to his service in China, just before and after the famous Siege of the Legations.

Countless articles, books and memories were published on this bloody episode, often using tones which are unpalatable to modern readers, full of chauvinism and racism. For this reason, the sincerity of this detached diplomat and his

---

4. *The vanquished promise victory to the unvanquished.*

frugality of words is indeed refreshing.

Salvago Raggi's pages are full of wit and possess historical relevance, shedding light on some hitherto unknown historic details, like the murder of the German Minister, Ketteler. After the telegraph lines were cut, in July 1900, a sort of media frenzy took over the world, and false news began to spread, like the rumor that all the people locked inside the Legations quarter had been massacred by the Boxers. The first obituary of the murder of Giuseppe Salvago Raggi and his family appeared in Italy on 22 July 1900, in the illustrated magazine *Illustrazione Italiana,* and in Italian churches prayers were offered for their souls.

The emotion created all over the world by those events ran so deep that even after the horrors of WWII, in 1963, Hollywood managed to release a blockbuster movie based on this subject. The film's title was *The 55 days of Peking* starring Charlton Heston, Ava Gardner and David Niven. In it the Americans are presented as the main actors of the defense of the Legation quarter although, according to Salvago Raggi, their role had been marginal.

The memoirs of Giuseppe Salvago Raggi were first published in 1968, as an appendix to the book of Glauco Licata *Notabili della Terza Italia* and a second time in 2011, as an independent volume under the title of *Ambasciatore del Re. Memorie di un Diplomatico dell'Italia Liberale.*

Slight changes have been made to the original text, adapting, whenever necessary, the transliteration of Chinese names into *pinyin* and Western names into their modern rendering, like Heyking instead of Hey King, Sir Claude MacDonald instead of Sir Claude Mc Donald, Great Britain instead of England and so on. All the French sentences are left without a translation, on the assumption that cosmopolitan readers would understand.

Notes taken from a script left by Pippo's wife, Camilla

Salvago Raggi Pallavicino have also been inserted, perhaps written on the ship taking her back to Italy after the Siege. Only twenty pages remained, ten having been torn out and there is no indication of who, or why, this was done.

All credit is due to Camilla Salvago Raggi, Pippo's beloved granddaughter and a writer in her own right, who spent her youthful years together with her formidable grandfather. She has lovingly preserved his written pages, which were recently moved for safekeeping into the Library of the Senate in Rome.

I wish to thank Gail Taylor, formerly of HKPolyU for revising and correcting my English translation.

Angelo Paratico

I

After two years of direct communication, several of the British officers in Egypt, like Kromer, Kitchener[5], Wingate, Gorst, Palmer and so on, thought it easier and more natural to continue speaking unofficially with me, since I knew already what was going on there, rather than with my newly appointed superior, Minister Tupini. But when I related to him their words, I had the distinct impression that he was upset, feeling that he was not sufficiently considered. I told him, quite frankly, that if he thought it better not to have as secretary a man who had been for too long *chargé d'affaires* there, then he should inform the Ministry, because even if I was enjoying my stay in Cairo, I had no wish to remain if he saw a problem with it. I am convinced that Tupini wrote privately about this matter, because I was authorized to leave *sans esprit de retour*.

On reaching Rome I had a meeting with Bonin, the undersecretary of State, further discussing the content of Tupini's letters but without any progress.[6]

I went then to Campale, where my family was staying.

---

5. In 1894 Giuseppe Salvago Raggi was appointed Secretary of the Legation of Italy at Cairo. Lord Cromer, Evelyn Baring, who was a cousin of Randolph Churchill, was Consul at Cairo from 1883 until 1907 and died in 1917. Sir Elwin Mitford Palmer (1852–1906). Lord Horatio Herber Kitchener (1850-1916), was governor of Sudan. He commanded the war against the Boers (1899-1902) and was minister of War in 1914. General Sir Francis Reginald Wingate (1861 – 1953) was a British general and administrator in Egypt and the Sudan. Sir Eldon Gorst (1861 – 1911) was Consul-General in Egypt from 1907-1911.

6. Lelio Bonin Longare (1859-1933). After the 'imaginary' victories of Coatit and Senafè but before the disaster of Adowa, the Italian Ministry of Foreign Affairs sent some ambitious instructions to Cairo, ordering to help the British in their occupation of Sudan, then get a share of it. Salvago Raggi wisely left those letters in his drawer, disregarding them. When Tupini found them, he was shocked by the fact that Salvago Raggi had ignored his superiors' instructions.

After a few days, I received a telegram, recalling me to Rome and on reaching our Capital, Count Bonin told me that our minister in Beijing, Bardi[7] had died and the Foreign Ministry wanted to show me gratitude by offering that position 'for my services in Cairo' as he kindly put it. Then he added that he considered that a favor done to me and, therefore, if I thought otherwise, I was free to refuse my appointment if I thought that the position was not convenient. My reply was: "I do accept it".

I had the impression that my answer surprised the undersecretary of State, who added that the Legation was temporarily in the hands of the interpreter, and because of this it was important to depart at once, but I could take a few days to think about his offer before giving him a firm answer.

I went to take my breakfast and I thought about it. I then become convinced - perhaps I suspected that there was too much of Machiavellianism at the Ministry - that to disentangle themselves from the promise of compensation they had made to me, not knowing how to calculate it, since I told them I wanted nothing, they had thought to offer me a position of *chargé d'affaires*, a high position in view of my youth but not so appealing, considering the distance and the uncomfortable location, especially for those, like me, with a family. My expected: "No, thank you" would have closed that comedy of give and take. Being this the conclusion of my thoughts, the only option left for me was to accept. I went to Cook to check when the first boat to Shanghai was sailing and there, and I learned that the *Prinz Heinrich* of the Lloyd Nordentscher line was departing from Genoa in seven days. I returned in the afternoon to see Bonin, telling him that I would depart on the following Wednesday. My decision greatly surprised him, and he kindly enquired if my wife was happy to follow me over there. I answered that I was unaware

___

7. Alessandro Bardi (1855-1896).

of what my wife wanted to do but I knew that I was going. Bonin told me that the Minister wanted to see me and I visited him a little later.

I had not seen Minister Visconti Venosta[8] since I was a young boy at Alfieri's home. He spoke to me very courteously and he asked if I was aware of what the Ministry was doing for me, by offering the position of Italy's *chargé d'affaires* in China to such a young secretary like me. Despite the cordial reception of the esteemed Minister, I was somewhat taken aback by the question, particularly so since I had planned for my departure and I had not complained about the destination. He was trying to present to me that appointment as a promotion, which was in fact a bad offer. I answered that I never discuss the orders from the Ministry as I had already demonstrated with my quick acceptance and even quicker planning for my departure, without complaining about the destination. Had the Ministry wanted to offer me something special, then sending me to Beijing, with the prospect of staying in charge there for two or three months at most, and then being replaced by a real minister of the Legation, leaving me as a Legation's secretary was not quite what I expected. That would have been suitable for a secretary of second class with a couple of years of experience, but that did not look very appealing to me, when compared with the career prospects of colleagues of my age and experience who were now posted in Europe. Even in Cairo, I was in a better position.

Marquis Visconti then promised that I would be left in charge until the Spring of 1898, save for unexpected circumstances, and then he would have me recalled upon the arrival of a new minister. I thanked him for giving me such guarantees, even though I realized that a Foreign Affairs Minister seldom can ensure the conditions of a diplomatic post, therefore I did not think that his promise was binding.

---

8. Emilio Visconti Venosta (1829-1914). Minister of Foreign Affairs (1863-64). Then again in 1896 and finally in 1899-1901.

But I learned to my great surprise, two years later, that on leaving his cabinet post he briefed his successor about the promise he had made to me. The fact that he informed his successor of the promise made to a young secretary shows that Visconti Venosta was a true gentleman. Two years later, because of some differences between the two of us, which had caused him some consternation, I believe, he regretted his decision to have me posted to China. I am sure that he was upset because, having met me at a public event, he responded with intentional coldness to my salute. But I shall return on this later, to explain such matter.

We sailed at the beginning of April: my father and I could get only closed cabins, where he suffered from heat and lack of ventilation.

At Port Said, Muhammad, my former butler who I had placed as *cavass* (porter) at

the diplomatic agency in Spain came to ask me if he could accompany us, even though he realized that he would get a lower salary than he was getting in Cairo. Only on two or three occasions had I seen persons in my service demonstrating such devotion, this being one.

Even Sforza[9] came to tell me that if I could get the appointment for an adjutant, he would gladly join me. But I had no opportunity to ask for one and I would have not asked for him; although I had never felt any dislike for him, the point was that I never appreciated his fatuousness.

We reached Shanghai in May, where I rested for a few days and then departed again, boarding the King Sing of the Jardine & Matheson Company, bound for Tianjin. In those days, such voyages were made with small ships, devoid of

---

9. Count Carlo Sforza (1872-1952). Italian Foreign Minister, 1947-1951. Minister of Foreign Affairs in 1920-21. Ambassador to Paris in 1922. He refused to work with Mussolini and went into exile from 1927 until 1943.

comforts. In Shanghai I met Leo Ghisi[10] our honorary consul and in his office, I was introduced to Mr. Angelo Luzzatti[11], who announced that he would be travelling to Beijing soon, where, he said, had important business to attend.

On reaching Tianjin we met our interpreter, Baron Vitale[12], who had come to welcome me. He was a very odd young man, gifted with an extraordinary genius for languages but with a level of absent-mindedness and distraction even more remarkable. Such a complexity of qualities and deficiencies made him a precious colleague on one hand and a useless one on the other.

Alberto Pansa[13]told me, and later Vitale confirmed it, that when the Ministry announced the arrival of a young man of 22 or 23 years of age who "knew Chinese and 5 or 6 other languages" he was quite skeptical, and as soon as he saw him entering his study he called the boy and asked the interpreter to tell him something. Vitale spoke using his best Chinese and..., the boy went to call the head-boy, because he could speak English. A skeptical smile appeared on Pansa's face and desolation on Vitale's, who then summoned his wit to say that he could not understand why the boy was unable to understand what he was telling him. He then asked the Minister if he had a text in Chinese of which he knew the translation, since he was ready to demonstrate his skills by translating it, and then he would be convinced that he could

10. Was a rich Italian businessman and honorary Consul of Italy, and his former villa is still visible in Shanghai in Yueyang Lu.

11. Angelo Luzzatti was a relative of Luigi Luzzatti, Prime Minister of Italy in 1910. Apparently, he shared some of the negative characteristics of his nephew, which Salvago Raggi discussed as recorded in the following pages.

12. Guido Amedeo Vitale (1872-1918) survived the Siege but died in Naples while drinking a coffee in a bar, accidentally shot by two criminals.

13. Alberto Pansa (1844-1928) was Italy's representative in Beijing (1889-1892) and in Berlin (1907-1911). Salvago Raggi had worked with him in Cairo in 1894 and commented in his memoirs that he was 'the man I respected most among those I met during my career'.

indeed translate it from Chinese. Pansa had on his desk a note translated by the interpreter of the British Legation: he passed it to Vitale who, after a quick look, translated it into Italian, while the minister was following the Englishman's translation. That greatly increased the value of the young linguist, who, following Pansa's advice, went to live for a few weeks in the Chinese quarters of the city and then returned, speaking perfectly the Mandarin he had studied in Naples with a professor who had only a classical knowledge of it, but was unable to pronounce it correctly. A couple of months were enough to correct his shortcomings and Vitale became, as I said, an excellent translator. On the other hand, he was fluent in Russian, Manchu, Mongol, English, French, German, Spanish, Dutch, Arabic, Turkish and, during his staying in Beijing, he managed to learn Finnish. I forgot to mention that he could read Latin and Greek as if he had

From Left: Ma Jianzhong, Sabbione, Angelo Luzzatti, Benvenuti, unknown.

just left High School. Strange to say he ignored Japanese, the only language which could have been useful to him in Beijing, besides Chinese.[14]

The railway line at that time did not go as far as Beijing, so we had to alight twenty kilometers from the Capital, and then my family completed the journey by sedan-chair while I rode on horseback.

We reached the Legation at around four in the afternoon and I found our house completely empty of furniture. I had asked the Ministry to send a telegram instructing those remaining not to sell the furniture of Minister Bardi, but instead, they had prepared a letter, and... that letter was travelling with me. Vitale had forgotten to mention it while we were in Tianjin, where I could have left my family temporarily behind, lodged in a hotel. It is not very pleasant to find yourself in a house totally empty with a lady, an old man, a child and two servants at four in the afternoon in a city where there are no shops selling furniture, or hotels. I was fortunate to find in Beijing the Baroness von Heyking[15], an old acquaintance of mine since my time in Cairo, who had left a welcome card and an offer to help.

The wife of the British Minister, Lady MacDonald[16] who I had never met before, wrote to me: "Dear Sir, I am aware that you have no furniture, so if you need three beds, some chairs, some tables, three tubs and three basins, please send somebody to pick them up."

That was how I spent my first days. A dash to Tianjin in the following days allowed me to return to the Legations of

---

14. Ambassador Daniele Varè, who met Vitale in Beijing in 1913, wrote that he added Japanese to his linguistic repertoire. He also noted his oddity and his childishness. Varè and his wife enrolled him as a teacher of Mandarin, but he proved useless, since: "He just lies back in his chair and laughs at us. Especially when we mix up the tones."

15. Elisabeth von Heyking (1861-1925)

16. Ethel MacDonald (1857-1941)

Germany and Great Britain the beds, the chairs, the tubs and the basins.

I think that those who visit Beijing today have no idea of what the Capital of the Middle Kingdom was like at that time. Laying in a flat and arid plain, in that season burned by the sun, devoid of a blade of green grass, there appeared on the horizon some high yellowish walls, dark, perfectly straight, smooth, and with no battlements.

A large caponier masked the gate of the Chinese City and we had to enter in it from the two side openings. After that gate, we found ourselves in a large plain, partly cultivated and partly not, with clusters of houses and a country road crossing them, covered with grey dust 40 or 50 cm high. Wanting to get home quickly, we proceeded at a gallop, even if I was afraid that the horses would stumble on stones concealed by the dust, or in a channel; fortunately, Chinese horses, stocky and graceless though they may look, are very robust.

Going forth, the houses became more and more packed and we reached new walls, taller and better built. Through the usual kind of caponier we entered the Tartar City, where the road was even more dusty and raised on the margins, so that what we would call sidewalks were three palms lower than the road. The track was flanked by low walls, interrupted here and there by a small roof or a door covered with a canopy.

When Vitale told me that it was Legation Road, I thought he was joking: there were no houses; but he explained to me that the abodes of the people were to be found behind the walls, and he then pointed to the gates of the Legation of Russia, Holland and the United States of America. We then reached a large bridge without railings under which was flowing, or should have been flowing, the water of a canal but at that time it was nearly dry; nevertheless, right there I saw some green grass, the first since I had entered Beijing.

The horses kept galloping in two or three palms of loose

dust, dark, with the so-called road flanked by walls behind which, as Vitale told me, the Legations of Spain, Japan and Germany were concealed. Then a large gate appeared, covered with shiny green shingles in front of which were two monstrous lions of white-yellowish limestone: that was the entrance of the French Legation. Further down there was a modest gate and that was the Italian Legation into which we made our entrance.

There was a single floor building, with a verandah and a small courtyard which was dividing the road from the building. To the right and to the left were two small yards with two low houses: the one on the left was for the interpreter and the one on the right for the secretary. The general impression was distressing.

Polly Condit Smith

II

In Beijing nine nations were represented. The English representative was Sir Claude MacDonald[17] who had been a career army officer, reaching the grade of Major. He proved to be an excellent colleague. Tall, thin, with long reddish moustache; rather intelligent, frank, loyal, polite and generally good humored. Lady MacDonald was a Scot, like her husband, about forty years old: tall, with regular facial traits, curt manners but likeable, cordial, a good woman, good with all, but she ended up quarrelling with Baroness von Heyking when the relations between England and Germany were at a low ebb. The von Heykings, who I knew already, were very kind to us, even when their relations with the MacDonalds were strained. It seemed to me that their kindness toward me improved with a plan, perhaps, to get me on their side. The Minister of France was then Auguste Gerard[18], a learned man, despised by all, ill-mannered and not at his best in society, who had been a 'lector of Empress Augusta'[19].

Mr. Denby,[20] the minister of the United States, was the classic American. Tall, clean shaven, he was a happy drinker of whisky, which he offered at any hour of the day to all those who visited him.

A story circulated that, soon after his arrival in Beijing, a young chancellor attached to the French Legation, Mr. Le Duc went to see Denby who, after listening to his name, mistook it for a Duke and invited the newly arrived fellow to

---

17. Sir Claude MacDonald (1852-1915).

18. Auguste Gerard (1852-1922). In Beijing from 1893 until 1897.

19. Augusta von Sachsen-Weimar-Eisenach (1811-1890).

20. Colonel Charles Denby (1830-1904).

lunch where Gérard was also present. At the time of sitting down the 'Duke' was offered the arm of Lady Denby, and this caused him a fair amount of consternation, which gave place to embarrassment when they asked him to sit on the right of the lady of the house, while the Minister was put at her left.

One year later Denby was replaced by Conger.[21] While Cassini,[22] the minister of Russia had left when I arrived and the Legation was in the hands of Alexandr Ivanovich Pavlov, a Russian of the bourgeois, not very kind, not very liked. During the Russian-Japanese war, he was caught helping himself to funds intended for the military, together with an accomplice, the military attaché de Wogato.

The Minister of Belgium was Baron de Wint, who was still young, also courteous, but indifferent.

A wonderful character was Cologan,[23] the Minister of Spain. Very tall, thin, with a scarce gray beard, pleasant, not devoid of intelligence but of no culture, disorderly and disinterested in the business, which anyway was non-existent in his Legation. One day he sang the praises of his archival system, which he had reduced to a maximum of simplicity. On his desk, on the right side, were the papers he had to answer; in the waste basket those he had answered. Following this system very little remained to do for his secretary, and it was better like that because the good Mr. Solivares, a little old man over sixty, forgotten for reasons unknown, as secretary of the Legation in Beijing, was a complete incompetent. I believe he was born like that for, in all the years of his diplomatic career, he had been unable to learn French, and he was entertaining the diplomatic corps with his blunders. One day he wrote to a young Belgian lady: "Si vous voulez

---

21. Edward Hurd Conger (1843-1907).

22. Arturo Paul Nicholas Cassini, Marquis de Capuzzuchi de Bologna, Count de Cassini (1836–1913).

23. Bernardo J. de Cólogan y Cólogan (in Beijing 1895-1902) he was the doyen among the Ministers.

faire un plaisir a un vieus lard, venez diner chez moi tel jour à 8 heures, deshabillé, c'est Mme Untel e Mme Untel qui l'ont demandé." All that was because the two ladies, being summer, had observed that the guests should come wearing a canvas jacket instead of a formal dinner jacket.

While Cadogan had gone to Japan to visit his brother, who was a military attaché there, Solivares was left in charge. One morning they announced his visit, while I was shaving at 8 in the morning. I asked him to wait and I quickened my toilette to see what he wanted at such an early hour.

He then announced the assassination of Canovas del Castillo, explaining that he had rushed to tell me first because the murderer was Italian.[24]

The Minister of Holland was Mr. Knobel[25], a despicable character who, while secretary in Teheran, had wedded a French girl, the daughter of a shopkeeper who, I don't know why, was trading in Persia. The poor Lady Knobel, ugly, undistinguished, good, talkative, could have been quite likeable but she was mistreated by her brutish husband who abused her with his revolting manners.

Besides the diplomatic Corps there were in Beijing the employees of the Imperial Chinese Customs. The creator of that wonderful organization was Sir Robert Hart[26], an Irishman, already seventy years old who had arrived more than forty years earlier in Beijing as a junior interpreter at the Legation. On reaching the level of Consul he was detached by the English Government to the Chinese one and tasked with the creation of that administration on which, when I was in Beijing, not only the Customs depended but also the

---

24. Antonio Cánovas del Castillo (1828-1897) served six terms as Spanish Prime Minister. Murdered by the Italian anarchist Michele Angiolillo.

25. Philip Fridolin Marinus Knobel (1857-1933). Dutch Minister 1895-1901

26. Sir Robert Hart, 1st Baron, (1835-1911) served as the second Inspector-General of China's Imperial Maritime Custom Service (IMCS) from 1863 until 1911.

Post, the Telegraphs, the Ports, the Light Towers, and in short, all public services.[27]

The administration was working extremely well because Sir Robert had a talent in organizing it well and he knew how to keep it on the right path but, by then, he was just an old maniac. His wife, tired of Beijing and her husband, had left ten years earlier and had not returned. In spite of it he did not allow anybody to move even a chair inside his wife's sitting room, which was open only when there were parties. From one of her old blue skirts, he kept cutting stripes of silk to be used as ties, which he was always wearing and were becoming narrower and narrower with the passage of time, since the raw material was becoming increasingly scarce. Sir Robert was known as a great China hand but, as will be explained later, when the Boxer disturbances began he did not understand much of it and, like us, he could not forecast anything, not even a few days before the Siege, even though his home was close to the Legations.

The social life in Beijing was similar for all of us. We were like country gentry of a region completely isolated from the rest of the world. We met often and we regularly ate in each other's company. We usually met at the Club, which was a small house with a room where illustrated magazines were provided, and there were two tennis courts which were flooded in winter and transformed into ice skating rinks.

It was impossible to stroll in the streets: dust changed into mud and, since the sewage was not functioning properly, the roads became muddy to the point that moving was impossible. In summer the diplomats went up to the temples. In the past centuries, Buddhist temples had been built on the hills, twenty kilometers from Beijing, and the bonzes rented rooms to the diplomats, who took their field beds, their tubs, and their dishes with them, camping among monstrous

---

27. By 1899 it employed 993 foreigners (503 were British) and 5.000 Chinese.

looking Buddha, while letting the months of July and August go by, months in which the city was half flooded and smellier than usual.

Beijing had, earlier than the European cities, created a perfect sewage system, indeed a beautiful system, tall and spacious, where a man could walk inside; an office was also created to take care of them, and it was prescribed that an appointed high officer should inspect them personally, once a year, to make sure that they were perfectly maintained. To prove that point, he would ask one of his employees to enter from one side, and he would wait for his exit on the other side, thus demonstrating that the sewer was walkable. All had been arranged by the careful Chinese legislator, but the employee who was pocketing the money not spent on maintenance was smarter. It was enough to give a tip to the porters of the high officer and they would take a longer road, while the employee would jump out of the entrance and walk on the surface to reach the exit. When he came within sight of the inspector, both pretended that all had been properly done, because they were sharing the profit. The entire Chinese administration was organized and worked like that. The institutions were perfect on paper, yet their functioning was deplorable, because of the corruption or the *squeeze* as they called it in Oriental English. All the Chinese - from the humblest servants to the Princes - squeezed the State and the family like a lemon. Salaries were ridiculously low but the profits huge. Those who looked at the practical results had the impression of ruin: those who studied the book of the laws stood in wonder and admiration.

Nothing was more laudable than the office of the Hanlin - the censors! A certain number of old functionaries with white hair, who knew the laws by heart, were nominated censors. They were supposed to renounce all promotions, and all honors. They were informed of all proposals submitted to the Emperor, and their task was to survey and discover problems, then inform the Emperor, to whom they directed their recommendations - without any minister interfering - about what could be useful or damaging to the Empire. They were the guardians of the State... in fact, anybody who wanted to propose something to the Emperor had to *buy* them first.

Those who had seen China at the end of the XIX Century could form a clear idea of how the great empires of Assyria, Babylon and Persia worked: an imposing machinery based on the legislative procedures and traditions on which they were founded, but which had become brittle because of corruption, to the point of crumbling at the first strike. In those empires, like China, the State was kept together by bureaucratic customs: a traditional religious respect made scores of officials *kowtow* in front of a sovereign who looked down on them unperturbed from his throne. To appear in front of them, he had to leave his harem, and then stood immobile like an idol and received homages. While they, having completed their traditional rites, returned to their provinces where satraps, viceroys or *tao-tai* governed half-independent entities, and separated by the rest of the empire, they considered themselves as Viceroys of the North.

The Viceroys of the North were surprised when, during the war with France, the French Admiral did not limit himself to fight in the South, and they said: "That man is at war with the South! What is he doing here?" And they were startled on hearing the cannons of the French warships.

China had remained the Asiatic empire of antiquity. The same country, which had a civilization when Rome was a small village, had handled gun powder when in Europe we were fighting with arrows; had invented paper money, when we were starting to use promissory notes, the great empire of Cathay, which had impressed the Venetian Marco Polo, although he knew Constantinople. Such a large Empire, yet one which had remained frozen in its institutions and nibbled at by woodworms, was slowly collapsing and presented to Europeans an image like that which we would have encountered in Egypt if those temples, instead of being used as dwellings, had been left intact but without maintenance and slowly decaying.

China would have been like the Babylonian empire if that had survived, standing without transforming, without renewing. And the Chinese had a mentality like their institutions.

After the war with Japan I read in the century-old Beijing Gazette: "The 'Eastern vassals' (the Japanese) had dared to revolt. The great Emperor, son of Heaven, had sent his soldiers, his ships, to scare them and persuade them to return to obedience: but they were so wicked that instead of bowing in front of the imperial banners, had dared to kill the soldiers of the Middle Kingdom. Horror! The good sovereign, not wanting to expose his loyal soldiers to the danger of a fight, had called other barbarians from the West. Looking at them, the Japanese rebels were struck by terror and implored the son of Heaven to be pardoned - and he, in his great clemency, had granted it."

That was their official version. Did they really believe it? I cannot say, but this was the official narrative dictated by the Emperor, and no one wanted to discuss it.

When a Chinese minister had an official conversation with me which he did not like, he inspected my watch, surprised that I had only one, contrary to the Chinese, habit and he asked me if the watch was male or female. Did he really believe that watches had different sexes? I don't know, but the habit of educated people dictated that watches should go in pairs, therefore one had to be male and one female. It was not for polite people to doubt it or even discuss it.

Chinese accepted virtually all religions. They were Buddhists, Confucians, and Taoists. One day I demanded a punishment for some Chinese who had sacked a Catholic Mission; a minister asked what they had damaged, and I answered: sacred images. When he learned that they had destroyed an image of the Holy Mary, he exclaimed that those people ought to be punished severely because *Ma-là* (Mary) was a very powerful goddess. Then he added to the Buddha of the Lamas and to the idols of the Taoists also the *Ma-là* of the missionaries. But to follow all religions means not to follow any, and in effect, the Chinese had no religion. They were just following rituals and protocols. It was enough for an imperial decree establishing the Republic to see the political-religious imperial structure fall. In 1899 China was going to fall asleep once more in her little opium bed, from which she had been woken up during the war with Japan.

Li Hongzhang[28], without realizing that he was involuntarily committing plagiarism, was in favor of a policy like that of Abdul Hamid[29] and was happy to see the European powers intervene, being jealous of Japanese expansionism and afraid of their encroachment after the Sino-Japanese war.

But neither the old Li, nor the Emperor and the mild Prince Qing, used to deal with the 'Western devils' could imagine that those same devils, after having contained the Japanese, wanted to nibble away at the territory of the empire.

Back then the Chinese had in front of them only a few quiet months.

---

28. Known as Li Hung-chang (1823-1901), he was a Chinese politician, general and diplomat of the late Qing dynasty. He quelled several rebellions and served in several important positions at the Qing Imperial Court, including that of Viceroy of the province of Zhili.

29. Abdul Hamid (1842-1918), Sultan from 1887, dethroned by the *Young Turks* in 1909.

III

I was not yet officially installed in my position when Angelo Luzzatti arrived in Beijing. Today, no one remembers this gentleman but at that time he had a certain degree of notoriety and they were talking about him in Rome, and even more in Florence.

It seems that Luzzatti had a degree in engineering, but I don't know what he did when he was young; he confided to me that his parents were Jews. The first news about him in my possession dated back to about 1890, while he was in Siam, where he was granted a concession to mine rubies. I do not know if there were rubies but Luzzatti launched a mining company, sold the shares and took some losses. At that time, he asked the Italian Government to sign a treaty with Siam to guarantee his territorial integrity, and as a payment they would grant to Italy (but read Luzzatti...) some concessions. The Italian Government - at that time the Prime Minister was Rudinì and his son, Carlo, was a partner and friend of Luzzatti - granted him the official title of honorary minister and he was nominated Commander of the Order of St. Maurice, with permission to wear the uniform of the order. Then he wrote to minister Pansa to have his opinion on the proposed treaty (at that time the Minister based in Beijing was also in charge of Siam).

Alberto Pansa answered that to guarantee the territorial integrity of the King of Siam meant to step on the feet of England and France, the two colonial neighbors, which had already nibbled away at Siamese territory and were watching the rest with greed, held back only by mutual suspicion and jealousy. He believed the advantage that Italy would derive from such a treaty, by giving concessions to Mr. Luzzatti, would not make up for hurting the aspirations of France and England and, anyway, before any move could be made, discussions should be held with those two countries.

The castle built by Luzzatti crashed down, but in the meantime, he had sold his shares and had moved elsewhere. He came to China and I never understood why and how he came to know Ma Jianzhong. [30]Perhaps the opportunity to move to China was given to him by Carlo Rudinì. Perhaps freemasonry was involved but I have no proof or news to support such an idea.

Ma Jianzhong was a Christian, but he must have broken all contacts with his congregation. He entered the Chinese bureaucracy with a recommendation from Li Hongzhang and was appointed Chinese representative in Korea. Afterwards, he dealt officially with the *China Merchant's*, a company controlled by the government, rather similar to the Italian state-owned enterprises. In that position, he had a great fall from grace: somebody with whom he was on bad terms accused him of stealing and he was dismissed. This accusation, made in a country where everybody is stealing would not normally have carried much weight, which suggests that he must have wronged a powerful adversary, although not to the point of upsetting Li Hongzhang, who remained his friend.

Luzzatti must have discussed a lot of things with Ma Jianzhong during a trip they made from Shanghai to Beijing in 1895-96. The result of these conversations was that Italy would return to China with the support of British finance and provide a certain amount of cash, to be used for the usual *squeeze*. Ma Jianzhong assured Luzzatti that *something will be done*.

Luzzatti, following the program they had set the year before, had returned forthwith, after having set up in Great Britain the *Peking Syndicate* with a capital of 40.000 Pounds,

---

30. Ma Jianzhong, Tientsin's taotai and secretary of Li Hongzhang.

if I remember well, represented by 30.000 shares valued at one pound each and 10.000 valued at one shilling. The last were privileged shares to be exchanged into the equivalent shares of one pound when the great company they were dreaming of would be launched.

What the business of the great company would be no one knew, including Ma Jianzhong and Luzzatti!

Luzzatti was a corpulent Jew of medium height, with a wavy black beard, completely bald, his eyes wide apart in his face, and he had manners typical of a rich Jew familiar with the ways of the world *where people are entertained*. To show his wealth, he was a big spender: he sported rings, flashy ties, gold cigarette holders embedded with stones, and he *behaved badly*. He had been endowed with a vivid imagination and a true geniality in launching new business. He knew little but understood everything. He made plans, which he abandoned in a split second, as soon as he noticed that they were not well accepted by his listeners and then he changed them into others, which he made up on the spot but which appeared to be the result of careful calculations.

In the diplomatic mail which I had received there was a dispatch from the Ministry with instructions for the accreditation of Luzzatti to the Legation, with words recommending him as the representative of a Syndicate, which was aiming to obtain wide concessions in China. They added that Luzzatti was also credited with the British Legation in Beijing, because the Syndicate was Anglo-Italian.

During our preliminary conversations, I asked what they expected to achieve, and he unfolded in front of me an admirable program, wide in scope and range. Luzzatti was thinking to ask about the possibility of setting up a Chinese State Bank with the rights of issuing banknotes. The Bank would have immediately offered a large loan to the Chinese Government, getting in exchange some monopolies, plus the concessions of the rights to build a railway from Beijing to Shanghai as well as establish mines in the Shantung region. I had the impression that they were selling the skin of a bear before killing it, furthermore they did not even know where the forest was in which the bear had his lair.

I asked the businessman if he thought that the Chinese government was really bent on creating a State Bank, something I was not aware of, and if they were willing to accept banknotes, something I saw as highly improbable, since there was no Chinese currency in the trade ports. Their currencies were the Mexican and Hong Kong dollars. In the Chinese hinterland, the currency was the silver ounce, the *tael*, which had to be weighed every time and finally, international monopolies would have created some insurmountable problems.

Luzzatti had an answer for everything. Between a cigarette and a Havana cigar, clipped with an elegant gold cutter, he would overcome all these difficulties. He did so with a flood of words which did not convince me, because they were just words.

He must have realized that, because he said that he would present Ma Jianzhong to me - 'a great gentleman' who coupled the knowledge of a great Mandarin with European culture. He would also present me an Englishman, I forget his name, who had accompanied him as the British side of the *Peking Syndicate*, while he, Luzzatti, represented the Italian side.

I learned on that occasion that the 'Italian side' owned a quarter of the share capital, attributed to Luzzatti as a compensation for his contribution... and for his ideas, and for of his work. The syndicate had put at his disposal 10.000 pounds for the expenses of his trip and his travels to China, with gifts for the mandarins, and he was keeping the remainder for his own private use.

The Englishman came and spoke little, nor did he appear

to be enthusiastic about his new colleague, and in fact, a few days later, he departed. Ma Jianzhong also came to visit me. He was a thin Chinese of medium height, who looked about fifty years old. With his small yellowish fingers, like the legs of a spider, he was rolling his cigarettes while explaining in strange French that the most important thing was to get the cooperation of those at Court. If that was achieved, then all could be arranged, and in this he was counting on the protection of Li Hongzhang and his ancient friendship with Pi Ha-li[31], an old eunuch who was very powerful, and very close to the Empress Dowager Cixi[32].

I must confess that a recent reading of an old dispatch by Pansa on the Siam's transaction proposed by Luzzatti had badly disposed me towards him and, without enthusiasm, I told them that I would consult first the representative of Great Britain, thinking that he should be as interested as me in the Syndicate, being Anglo-Italian.

When I did so, Sir Claude gave me a look which was not particularly enthusiastic, but it was not altogether skeptical. He told me that similar *brasseurs* were a common sight also for him. He did not know much about the projects of the *Peking Syndicate*, but he was prepared to gather information and, very kindly, said that he would be glad to cooperate with me.

During a second visit, Luzzatti told me that he had thought about my objections arising from the possible international complications for their demands for monopolies and he wanted to be presented to the German representative. He would then propose to get some German finance into the *Peking Syndicate*, and this would pre-empt German

31. Li Lianying (1848 –1911) was a Chinese imperial eunuch highly influential during the regency of Empress Dowager Cixi.

32. Empress Dowager Cixi (1835-1908) or Tzu-hsi of the Yehenara clan. She had been the concubine of the Xianfeng Emperor (reigned 1850-1861). They generated a male heir, the future Tongzi Emperor (reigned 1861-1875).

opposition.

I was impressed by the ease with which the Anglo-Italian syndicate was so quickly transformed into an Anglo-Italian-German one.

I introduced him to the German representative, and I noticed both the lack of preparation of that entrepreneur and the rapidity with which he could abandon one project and switch to a new one.

Baron von Heyking[33] listened carefully to the proposal of the *Peking Syndicate* and smiled at the mention of the creation of a State Bank and the issuance of paper money, but he wrinkled his eyebrows at the prospect of the railway and mines in Shantung. A few months later I understood the reason.

Then he asked Luzzatti why, instead of thinking about the Shantung's mines, which had perhaps already drawn the attention of some Germans, was he not considering mines in Shanxi, which were praised by Richtofen? Luzzatti thanked him for the advice but when we were out of the Baron's earshot, he asked me where Shanxi was, and who was Richtofen. I told him that Shanxi was a northern province, but I wasn't aware of a writer called Richtofen because my sudden calling to China had not allowed me time to fill the gaps in my knowledge of Chinese culture. That afternoon, Luzzatti was back in my office, and he looked radiant; he had found a copy of the Richtofen. The mines of Shanxi were wonderful. Ma Jianzhong was intimate with a close friend of the governor of that province. The State Bank, the banknotes, the mines in Shantung, were gone and forgotten now, he was sailing towards the coal mines of Shanxi and towards a railway. In less than 5 hours the plan had been turned! When later I informed Heyking, he looked glad. Then he could sleep quietly. No one would speak again about Shantung.

---

33. Edmund Friedrich Gustav von Heyking (1850-1915) was a German of Baltic origin.

An agent of Ma Jianzhong was dispatched to Shanxi and Luzzatti remained in Beijing. I often found him doing the rounds there, and I was resigned to suffer that *rasta*[34] because he represented the sole Italian interest in China.

In Autumn, after several trips made by the emissary of Ma Jianzhong and after several vicissitudes which I am not reporting here, Luzzatti had a contract signed in favor of the *Peking Syndicate* by the governor of Shanxi, who granted them all concessions on mines in the region and permission to build a railway. Luzzatti had achieved his goal but he had also managed to upset everybody in Beijing, especially those at the British Legation. The first interpreter, Cockburn,[35] had thrown him out of the door. He was also on bad terms with Sir Claude after a garden-party during which Luzzatti, present as a special envoy of the H.R.H. the King of Italy, and wearing his high uniform of the Order of St. Maurice, was caught embracing a British waitress behind a bush who, not willing to abandon herself to his attentions, had screamed for help.

Then his partners from London wrote back saying that the contract could have been the basis for a great business deal if it had the seal of the British Legation. Luzzatti felt sorry for the problem created with Cockburn and for the hugging of the uncooperative maid, which had put him in a bad light with Sir Claude Macdonald. When I asked Sir Claude about the seal, he told me that he would be glad to be my associate in promoting that Syndicate, since some of his countrymen in London were also in it, but he added that he did not want to have anything to do with 'that gentleman' whom he considered to be a 'swashbuckling.'

For a long time, I was asking myself what advantage

---

34. *Rasta* is a derogative term connected to Ethiopia. Meaning, at that time, a pest, a nuisance.

35. Henry Cockburn (1859-1927) Chinese Secretary at the British Legation.

that enterprise would give to Italy, and I frankly expressed my doubts to Luzzatti, who had begun to snub us until he realized that he needed the Legation's help. He then wrote me a letter promising that about a quarter of the future issuance of shares would be reserved to Italian capital, and that for all future enterprises in China a part would be reserved to Italy and Italian industry and personnel. He even sketched a flag for the *Peking Syndicate*, with a yellow background, but featuring the British and Italian flags. The flag seemed to me to be a minimal guarantee of the future advantages of Italian finance and labor but in my naivety, I was convinced that the Italian Ministry of Foreign Affairs had obtained a confirmation from the syndicate in London for what Luzzatti was guaranteeing to me, and that something would remain for Italy as a compensation for all my labor in helping that businessman.

I therefore wrote to the Ministry expounding upon all the precedents, plus my doubts and adding that, because of the bad impression received by the British Legation, their cooperation in the future would be limited so that Luzzatti had realized that he could only count on the help of the Legation of Italy. I explained that I had hopes that something good for Italy would come from what the *Peking Syndicate* would achieve but I added that the Government should seek a more solid guarantee of the kind mentioned in the letter which I was enclosing, and in the meantime, I was going to cease any action on the matter until I received telegraphic instructions from the Minister with the authorization to carry on. If that were the case then it would be possible to finalize something given the intervention of Ma Jianzhong and the secret approval of Li Hongzhang, who was asking whether we had forced his hand to put the Zongli Yamen's seal on the agreement.

In the meantime, Luzzatti was growing desperate and impatient because I was not moving a finger, and he could not visit the British Legation since its doors were forever shut for him, therefore he was tormenting me.

To gain some respite I called Luzzatti, reminding him that his personal situation was fragile because of the hostility of Sir Claude, and I could convince him to visit the Yamen with me only by telling him that Luzzatti was sorry. Therefore, he should move to Tianjin and stay there quietly for a month; then, I would let him know that it was possible to return. I set this date because my report has been delivered one month earlier and I was hoping that in two or three weeks I would get a reply. Luzzatti departed and I could breathe, while from Rome I received the order to help the *Peking Syndicate*. Hoping that the Ministry had obtained a serious guarantee in London, I approached Sir Claude, but found his attitude even colder than before, not only about Luzzatti but also about the *Peking Syndicate*. However, after some discussions, he did agree to write a note asking the Yamen to put their seal on the documents, and the next day I went to see the Chinese Ministers at the Yamen.

Since Li Hongzhang wanted 'his hand to be forced to put the seal', as Ma Jianzhong was claiming, I demanded that the Chinese Government accepted all that the Governor of Shanxi had accepted, and I prepared a project to which the Government was contributing seventeen clauses: I remember the exact number because I still vividly remember the meeting. The objections raised by the Chinese, and my insistence that the clauses be accepted, went on for a long time, while small cups of warm wine went around, poured from a small pan inside which the remaining drops were poured back again to be re-heated. Evening came while darkness fell; I had smoked a great number of cigarettes and I had a dry throat because of the long discussions. Finally, finding a way out, I proposed that they might at least put the seal of the Yamen on the contract, and then I would try to convince my own Government to endorse it. The Chinese

Ministers replied that it was too late already: the man in charge of the seal had already left. I asked them to send somebody to fetch it, but they answered that it was already dark.

"Switch on the lights" I told them, but there were no lights because at the Zongli Yamen no one worked during the night. I then lit my matches, putting them on the side of the desk. After half an hour, all my matches had been exhausted but the seal had been found, and I departed with the contract bearing the official seal.

I have explained the matter in detail - not because I want to claim a personal success, but because it gives an idea of how contracts were dealt with by four or five men, wearing embroidered silk, drinking warm wine, nibbling dry fruits and years' old eggs, while smoking water-pipes. This was the behavior of the Chinese Ministers, who picked their noses with small fragments of paper which were then deposited in small silver boxes they were carrying for that purpose, and emitted noises of obvious origin. As for me, I pretended to drink *saki,* but I was drinking a light tea, which I was beginning to like. In the meantime, I was praying to the prophet Job to lend me some patience while I smoked Egyptian cigarettes.

Of my success, there is no trace because Li Hongzhang wanted *his hand to be forced* but he was ready to sign the contract and then say that he had been forced to give way to the violence of that Western barbarians.

All this was conducted according to the customary protocol.

The European was a barbarian, an enemy, therefore nothing should have been granted to him, and a Chinese Minister who conceded anything was automatically losing his face; but the European, being a barbarian, had no education, and was a vulgar individual with whom it was impossible to hold a discussion in a civilized manner, following the Chinese etiquette. When that knave was beginning to demonstrate his gross manners, it was better to give him something and get him out of the way, because there was no point in carrying on a discussion with such a beastly person, so it was rather better to make him partially happy and let him go away. This was the Chinese logic. I am not pretending to be modest by declining to claim that the proceedings had been a success. There were no successes or abilities. They are considered so by the common people who see diplomats in the same light as jugglers who, at the right time, can catch a ball or a dish flying in the air, defeat their adversary and then cry victory. Nothing is further from the truth. In diplomacy, there is no success or *coup de main*. One may get positive results only by following a straight line of conduct, inviting a deal by *demonstrating that it is of reciprocal advantage* getting to an agreement and presenting a request at the right time.

In China, there was no diplomacy of this sort, there was only hugging with people who were still living in bygone years; and in my case I was aiding some adventurers.

Going home, coming from the Yamen, I paused at the British Legation to see Sir Claude who still was not aware of my contract with Ma Jianzhong and Li Hongzhang and was duly impressed by what I had achieved. I went to eat late but happy because I was convinced that I had assured a real Italian share of the participation in that capital formation, work and industry.

But no such shares materialized for Italy. Rudinì had written to the Ministry: "Let Luzzatti get help" and the great company was launched. Luzzatti, Carlo Rudinì and few other friends had shares; those of one pound went up to 24 or 25, then fell to 5 or 6 and I can't say what happened later.

I did manage to give employment to two Italians at the *Peking Syndicate* in Beijing, Sabbione and Benvenuti. One is dead and the other is in Italy, and I do believe that if the *Peking Syndicate* still exists, it has nothing Italian in it.[36]

36. It was an important deal. The British subscribers were Lord Rothschild and Carl Meyer. The newly formed company was unable to begin mining in Shanxi and they gave up their rights for redemption in 1908 for 2.750.000 taels of silver. The operations in Honan went on until 1923-1924, reaching a daily output of 4.000 tons of coal per day.

IV

I had already hinted before about the aims of Baron von Heyking over Shantung. The day when the German Minister had managed to divert the eyes of Luzzatti from Shantung to Shanxi I knew nothing, and I should confess that I did not notice anything. The doubt that my friend was handling something secret arose when he invited me for lunch at his residence where I found some special guests: some admirals of the German Navy. I found two officers in uniform and three dressed in civilian clothes; one of them could hardly see: he wore thick glasses, and I thought he was a doctor. The other was a hunchback. A hunchback in the German navy seemed rather peculiar to me. Much later Heyking told me that those two strange characters were port engineers who had come to China to study the setup of a bay which Germany had already decided to occupy. He then confessed to me, after having told me that they were Navy officers, that he felt bad, seeing an unexpected hunchback and noticing how I looked at that kind of *Triboulet*. He was a bit worried, and in the evening, he had told to his wife: "Salvago n'a pas avalé le bossu, qu' est que je le pourrais lui reconter?". The Baroness, who possessed great common sense, told him not to give me any explanation but let the matter rest. Later Heyking and the Baroness boarded a warship and toured the cost, reaching Shanghai. That jolly trip on a coast which offered no attractions did not convince me. The Baroness told me that they had conducted some interesting studies on the coast of Shantung. When, later, because of the accidental killing of a missionary, the occupation of Jiaozhou Bay was carried out, I asked the Baroness to show me the studies made before the occupation. All can still remember how, using that pretext, Germany took over Jiaozhou Bay, as Russia took over Port

Light Cruiser Marco Polo

Arthur, which a little earlier she had forced Japan to give back to China in exchange for a payment that China had not fully settled. France also followed suite, while, finally, Great Britain, unwillingly and in order not to lose face, was forced to occupy Wei Hai[37] just to neutralize the menace of Port Arthur and Jiaozhou against North China.

It was natural that such an epidemic of occupations awoke ambitions of imitation from all powers and, without being aware of it, my reports must have given the impression that we could also do something. But it was not my intention to suggest that, not because I hadn't entertained the same ideas but because, after thinking over it, I had concluded that it was neither justified nor useful for Italy to give it a try, because we were unprepared and because we had no interest at the Far East, which we ourselves were admitting by not having an Ambassador and where for years we had not stationed warships: in fact, after great efforts I was only able to call in the cruiser Marco Polo.

---

37. Weihaiwei remained British from 1898 until 1930, even if a part remained British until 1940. The leased territory had a surface of 288 miles. Port Arthur is known today as Lüshunkou.

In February 1898, I received a diplomatic dispatch from the Ministry in which there was a hint that we could imitate the other nations, and they solicited my opinion on this matter. I answered with a report which greatly satisfied me, because it appeared well balanced and apt to the situation. In a few words, I expressed the opinion that something could have been done if we had taken care of China before. Not to waste further time, and to be ready, I advised the Ministry to send one Consul to Shanghai and another to Tianjin, to set up a regular navigation line to Shanghai, then start to study the coastline, authorizing me to visit the southern provinces and then wait for the first chance.

The Rudinì-Visconti Government fell. Then the Foreign Affairs Ministry passed into the hands of Marquis Raffaele Cappelli[38], who took that office, if I am not mistaken, only for 17 days. In the meantime, he sent a note informing that my report had been received, and he praised it, then he wrote a line, wanting to: "Demonstrate his satisfaction for what I was doing in Beijing."

The next Foreign Affair Minister was Admiral Canevaro,[39] who was the brother of my cousin, Clorinda Migliorati but I had never met him. Soon after, I received a note, informing about the forthcoming arrival of a Minister of the Legation, Renato De Martino[40] who arrived, if I remember well, in September.

A few days before the arrival of the Minister of Italy, something had happened in Beijing and because of that the foreign representatives had decided to call a detachment of

---

38. Raffaele Cappelli was Foreign Affairs Minister from 1st to the 29 June 1898.

39. Felice Napoleone Canevaro (1838-1926). His father, Giacomo Canevaro, made a fortune in Peru, possibly trading also in Chinese coolies.

40. Renato De Martino (1843-?) had married a Swiss lady, Elisabeth De Wirsen. Their son, Giacomo De Martino (1868-1957) had a brilliant career as Ambassador in various capitals before WWII.

sailors to defend the Legations. Such incidents were not serious: my wife,[41]while going in a sedan chair at the Petang to see some Italian sisters, was made a target of threats. The bearers ran, entering a narrow lane, and their young *mafoo* (the groom) behaved with great courage, remaining behind to stop the assailants and, taking advantage of the narrowness of the road, was able to keep the menacing crowd in check by swinging his baton. Then he ran back to the sedan chair and they returned safely to the Legation without further incident. Even a Secretary of the United States legation was insulted and threatened in the Chinese city, close to the Tartar city.

After my complaints, the Chinese government behaved rather caringly but I sternly demanded that they send some ministers to present their excuses, pay the *mafoo* and to the porters I don't know how many silver taels and finally, that they should give a lower grade button to our brave *mafoo*. All these things were done. But the diplomatic corps, because of those incidents and others – as news of unrest were spreading – thought it better to ask for some detachments of marines, which they did, after having asked permission to their governments and having informed the Chinese government.

De Martino had boarded the cruiser *Marco Polo* in Japan, which was sailing to Tianjin to disembark some marines destined for Beijing.

Expecting that the Chinese Government would ask us not to call marines to Beijing and not wanting to have our representative entering the city together with those soldiers, I sent Vitale to Tianjin, advising De Martino to delay his visit to the Capital by one day. However, a telegram from the captain of the *Marco Polo* announced his arrival together with the soldiers. Clearly my advice had not been taken well.

I sent a sedan chair to the station[42] and then I went there

---

41. Camilla Salvago Raggi Pallavicini (1871-1915). They had a son, Paris Salvago Raggi (1892-1936) who was also in Beijing.

42. The rail terminus was at the station of Machiapu (Majuapu).

with some saddled horses, not knowing if De Martino was able to mount a horse. De Martino arrived and he was extremely kind, wanting to carry on the conversation with me while he was in the sedan chair and I was riding my horse, a thing not easy to achieve because of the narrowness and bad condition of the roads.

It was on that occasion that he told me that he was rushing to Beijing because we needed to proceed with the occupation.

"But occupation of what?" I asked.

And he answered: "Of a place we'll choose together with Captain Incoronato, who has the maps."

This short conversation remained engraved in my mind, perhaps because of the bad impression he gave me, due to the rush, total unpreparedness and stupid planning he wanted us to follow. I remember that I moved ahead of the sedan chair brooding over what I had just heard.

After lunch, we met Captain Incoronato of the warship *Marco Polo* who had already placed some nautical maps on the table. Then we looked at the coastline of Pecili, which had limited interest, indeed it would have been a folly to even think about, even if there were good ports. After the ports of Shantung and Shanghai, we evaluated Nimrod, Sanmen Bay and then Samsah. We concluded that those three were the only possible places. It is useless to reveal here the flippancy with which we were looking at those maps in Beijing, which could have been studied before leaving, while in Rome. Nevertheless, the captain received instructions from the Minister to depart and visit those places, and then report back.

Then, noticing my bad mood, which had greatly increased because of the way in which events had unfolded, De Martino delivered a long and unctuous speech, full of praise for me, and he mentioned my report, sent in March which he called *wonderful,* adding that my only mistake had been to throw water on the fire. I was, he said, right, in theory, in recommending preparedness but in so doing no action could be taken and he concluded by adding that: "Italy needs to be pushed, not hold back: when our Nation is at high sea, it sails, but woe betide to let her proceed with caution."

Since I remained silent, he carried on: "And now let's come to you. The Ministry knows that you had received a promise to be recalled once a proper Minister would be appointed here in Beijing; therefore, you should have already been recalled, but I have insisted on keeping you here. I would be glad to have your collaboration; here great things will be accomplished. You have the right to be part of them and if you stay with me you indeed will be a part of them. You will be the one who will raise the Italian flag on the new Italian possession...".

I interrupted him, mustering my calm, by telling him that he should let the Ministry recall me, but he insisted, and then I told him that, frankly speaking, I did not wish "to be mixed up in what was going on here." My conclusion was not well received, even if I had delivered it with great restraint. De

View of muddy Peking in 1898

Martino stood up and he told me to prepare the telegram I wanted to send to the Ministry, then he went to discharge his repressed rage with Captain Incoronato.

The next morning, I showed him my telegram and he asked me to reconsider that matter for another day, since it was Friday and *he did not send telegrams on Friday*: but then, because of my insistence, the telegram was delivered with the addition of a kind sentence in the text, concerning my work, which that he had jotted down. The Ministry replied with my recall. Two days later De Martino departed. He left telling me that he was going for a hunt with Marquis Li, a son of Li Hongzhang, who owned lands in the Yangzi.

Then he gave me the address of a Dutch shopkeeper living in Shanghai, where I should direct all telegrams; he did not inform the Ministry of his absence and he told me that he would send me the telegrams to be ciphered and then to be forwarded to Rome. I looked at him in disbelief but, of course, I could not say anything.

After ten days all people knew, except me, that he had gone back to Tokyo to stay in a Japanese quarter with a Japanese lady.

When Captain Incoronato concluded his exploration in the three ports which were indicated (I seem to remember that it took him no more than 20 days!) he sent a telegram to the Legation, as follows: "First Samsah, then Nimrod, third Sanmen Bay. For the last one a lot of expenses will be needed." I believe I still remember the words of the telegram, but anyway, the sense of them was exactly this.

I transmitted it to the Minister through the appointed Dutch shopkeeper in Shanghai and two days later I received his answer, asking me to wire to Rome advising the Ministry to choose Sanmen Bay. I was convinced that there was a mistake and I sent a new telegram to the Minister, pointing out that according to Captain Incoronato the worst place was Sanmen Bay. I received a confirmation from him to indicate Sanmen Bay in the telegram, then I should put his name on it and have it sent henceforth with the Minister's signature. Given that I did not meet De Martino again I never understood the reason why he had taken that decision, against the best advice of Captain Incoronato.

A few months later, I had to wade into a violent discussion between Admiral Grenet and Captain Incoronato, because the first was accusing the commander of the *Marco Polo* to have indicated Sanmen Bay. I told him about the text of his telegram but, not believing me, I had to send him a copy.

Some days after sending this telegram and not seeing the Minister coming back I sent him a new message, always following the same route, telling him that the sailing season was closing (in Winter, when the river ices, all maritime links with Shanghai are cancelled) and I had to depart. De Martino replied with a telegram saying that I could leave, and he hoped to see me in Tianjin, because he believed that his boat was reaching Tianjin the day before my departure. I departed without meeting him and my boat was the last leaving Tianjin for that season. On the exit of the Taku port the boat on which the Minister was sailing in was close to mine going out and I saw him... Close to him there was a Japanese lady. Minister De Martino was about 60 years old!

I reached Shanghai where I met my wife who had travelled there on the cruiser Marco Polo, and as soon as I had reached her, I received a telegram from the Minister: "Great happenings are upon us, your presence in the Far East is necessary." I remember exactly the text because all that theatrical emphasis was greatly annoying, giving me a constant black mood. I replied that I had nothing to do in Shanghai and that, since Tokyo was also in the Far East, I hope that no difficulties would be raised for me to spend a few days over there. I received his permission, and I spent a month showing the country to my wife.

In January, I returned to Shanghai but nothing new had

happened in the meantime. I sent a telegram to Beijing, but it went unanswered, then I wrote to the Ministry in Rome and they answered to depart as soon as possible. I informed the Minister and I left Shanghai, if I remember well at the end of February 1899.

I went to Rome and the Minister of Foreign Affairs told me that he was working on the occupation of Sanmen Bay. I asked if the location had been decided and his answer was yes. He wanted to keep me in his council of advisers but because of a serious operation which my father had to undertake I went straight to Genoa, where I remained for a few days, without receiving further news from the Ministry.

The day on which my father had his operation, while they were putting him back in his bed, I received a telegram from the Minister asking me to return to Rome. I put it aside and I did not answer, and only later did I remember it. Again, two days later, the Minister, surprised at not having seen my answer, wrote again. I answered that I was assisting my father and I could not return to Rome.

Two days later, during my temporary absence from the clinic and assured by doctors of my father's recovery, by mistake he opened a third telegram directed to me: The Minister was, again, insisting to have me back. Since I was reassured in seeing my father sitting up in his bed and on the way of recovery and reassured by the positive comments from the doctors, I departed to Rome.

While on the train I read on the newspapers about our demand for Sanmen Bay and the sudden recalling of Minister De Martino. In Rome, the Foreign Affairs Minister, Admiral Canevaro, told me everything.

By then all comments were morphing into gossip. The Admiral asked me if it was true that De Martino was not in Beijing during the last period of my stay in the Chinese capital: I answered that he had told me that he was going hunting on the Yangzi with Lord Li, with whom he wanted to build a friendly relationship for the good of our mission. The Admiral demanded, then, if it was true that he had gone to Japan instead. I answered that to know the answer he should ask our representative in Japan, not me, since I had remained in Beijing. That was the end of our conversation. The next day the Admiral asked if I wanted to return at once to China. I refused, because I did not want to leave behind my sick father. Insisting, the Admiral told me that I would be promoted to Minister, adding that would be a great boost for my career (my rank was secretary of II class) but I refused, knowing well that my stubbornness was the equivalent of my resigning from the diplomatic service, but I thought that I

Giuseppe Salvago Raggi, wife Camilla and son, Paris, in Peking.

could not go. The Minister looked upset and told me that I should return to his office the next day. In the meantime, I had received some good news from my father in a telegram. The next day the Minister delivered a telegram to my address saying that he had sent a telegraph to my father, telling him about the good proposal he had made to me and asking him to write to me. The message from my father was "Do accept. Doctors assure me that in seven days I'll stand up."

I accepted the proposal. The Minister henceforth gave his instructions. A naval squadron, commanded by Admiral Grenet, would be sent composed of three warships: the *Calabria* from America would be moved to Shanghai, joining the *Marco Polo* and *Elba* already anchored there. Then we were going to despatch, just to add to the number, also the *Vespucci,* a ship used to train officers. In such a way, a sizeable naval squadron would add to the pressure on our demands and he was assuring me that the British and German Legations would support us. If the Chinese were going to refuse our demands for Sanmen Bay, we would then proceed with a forced occupation.

I was received by His Majesty King Umberto I, to whom, on his demand, I presented my thoughts, which were: *things had been decided with too much haste, without adequate preparation, and carried out in the worst manner; perhaps, it would had been better to let it slip away, but by now we had to succeed, otherwise we would lose our remaining prestige.*

Perhaps, with Sanmen Bay occupied, we could negotiate *an exchange* in order to give a sort of moral satisfaction to the Chinese.

His Majesty concluded that if the Minister had promised me that he would do as he said, then he was sure he would do it. But he could assure nothing else because all decisions rested with the Parliament. Those honest words were the last I heard from Umberto I: since I was not going to see him alive again!

I departed a few days later - if I remember well that was the 17 April 1899 - on the steamboat *Laos*.

On board, I had told nobody who I was and since the waiter in my cabin knew well Italian, there was no need to speak French, therefore all thought I could only speak Italian. That pleased me greatly, because I wanted to concentrate on my work, with no one disturbing me.

We were all immersed in the clamor of the Dreyfuss Affair[43] and in the first class were all French, who were divided into two warring factions, looking at each other with hostility. Sitting close to me *who did not speak French* all were chatting freely.

As soon as we reached Colombo and we were sitting at the table for lunch, I saw an Italian officer of our navy, who spoke with the maître, who told him: "Il n'y a aucun ministre d'Italie à bord." I stood up and went to the officer, who was Lieutenant Cantù. Admiral Grenet was in the same port and was expecting me for lunch. Then the anonymity had been lifted and for the rest of the trip I was no longer left in peace. I did not pick up secret confidences, but I spent some pleasant time with two officers of the French Navy and a colonel belonging to the French Army. From Shanghai I wanted to proceed to Beijing, but the cabinet crisis stopped me.

The Sanmen Bay affair and the Nerazzini Peace Treaty[44]

---

43. Alfred Dreyfuss (1859-1935). It was a political and judicial scandal which split French society between those who supported him and those who condemned him. In 1899, Dreyfus was taken back from Devil's Island in French Guyana for a new trial which resulted in a new conviction, but he was pardoned and set free. He was later rehabilitated.

44. Minister Cesare Nerazzini signed a Peace Treaty with the Negus, on 26 October 1896. After the Italian defeat of Adowa, the Italian occupation of Eritrea was accepted but the Italian Government renounced to it in order not to interfere with Ethiopia. About the Sanmen Bay affair, Italy did not intend to occupy military Sanmen Bay, after the opposition of Great Britain. Minister Felice De Martino made a blunder, due to a wrong sequence of telegraphic instructions he had received from Rome,

remain two sad pages in our national history. The bad influence of that peace is still casting its negative effects upon us. The Sanmen Bay affair no, it has been forgotten because, luckily, the Siege of the Legations made everybody forget it. That was my sole consolation during the black days in Beijing and we often returned to this point with Livio Caetani,[45] when we were almost sure of not getting out of it alive.

---

possibly sent by the same "scoundrel" who did not assign a progressive number to their messages, who then caused great embarrassment to Giuseppe Salvago Raggi during the signing of the Peace treaty with China. The author describes this episode it his last pages.

45. Livio Caetani di Sermoneta (1874-1915).

V

We reached Beijing, and it was there that I received the first great pain of my life: the death of my father. The day after I knew that I would never embrace my father again, I had to go to the Yamen. To get out of the Legation, seized as I was by such sorrow, to discuss with the Chinese, was the greatest sacrifice I have ever made for my service.

As it appears in the documents and contrary to the ministerial instructions which I had received, discussions on Sanmen Bay were never tabled again and when the Siege of the Legation happened, Italy had not renounced her claims: consequently, we could have started them again at any given time. I am not boasting of my old disobedience here: I don't know if I was right or wrong but for sure I acted - certain to be recalled and see my career end in ruin - convinced and in good faith that I was doing what was less disadvantageous for my Country, hoping that my successor would convince the new Foreign Affair Minister, Visconti Venosta or his successor, to decide something which was not up to me to decide.

I knew after the Siege that I had indeed been marked for a recall and only because of the progress of the disturbances was the recalling order not put into effect. This was a demonstration that intentionally I was acting against my best interests, and no one could accuse me of having disobeyed the orders because I expected a personal return out of it and this, after all, makes my lack of discipline looks lighter, albeit not entirely justifiable.

The stubbornness of the new Minister, Visconti Venosta, in recalling our warships in order to be able to announce to the Italian Parliament that we had renounced all our claims in China was such that he had ordered to the Admiral to return on the cruiser *Carlo Alberto* right when the Ministry was authorizing the Italian participation to a naval show of force put together by all the Powers, to convince the Chinese Government not to support the Boxers[46].

What I had told them, by sending letters and telegrams, about the disturbances in China was not believed, even if they could get a confirmation from the German Government, which had a representative who was far more pessimistic than myself. The situation then took a turn for the worst so quickly that the ships sent to help us were, I believe, in the Red Sea, when they met the ship carrying Admiral Grenet back to Italy. If they had not recalled him, I would have had 80 soldiers in Beijing instead of 40 and the deployment of the Italian forces would have been much more effective; with the Sanmen Bay expedition, instead of the 30 or 35 marines of Sirianni[47] we would have had one hundred or two hundred of them… But let's not complain too much! The few, with Paolini, did extremely well and the few, commanded by Sirianni, honored our Navy and let thanks be given to Heaven for that.

As I mentioned before, I was returning to China with the title of resident Minister. I had thus to present my credentials to the Emperor. I asked for an audience, and on the appointed day I departed from the Legation in a sedan chair directed to the Winter Palace, followed by our interpreter and Lieutenant Pignatti.[48] On reaching the Central courtyard I was received by the Prince and some ministers of the Yemen with Court officials. We crossed two halls and then we reached the lake, which we crossed on a boat, reaching a pavilion where the

---

46. Boxers was the English name of a Chinese secret society known as I-ho ch'üan, the *Righteous and Harmonious Fists*. They called the foreigners *Primary Hairy Men* and their program was to exterminate them and all the Chinese who sided with them.

47. Giuseppe Sirianni (1874-1955). Later Senator and Minister of the Navy, between 1929 and 1933.

48. Carlo Pignatti Morano (1869 –1944) later Admiral and Senator.

Emperor[49] was living. After a short wait in an empty hall, we were moved to the next where the Emperor was sitting on a high throne, reachable with lateral steps while in front of him was a table, where I was left standing.

Since the throne and the table were higher than the floor, every bow made by us, placed lower than the throne, made us disappear from the Emperor's sight; he may have thought that we had made the traditional *kowtow*, masking thus our grave deviation from the traditional Chinese etiquette.

I linger on such ludicrous details because, as it is well known to all those people who have studied the history of the relations between China and the European powers, long and difficult discussions were entertained to find an agreement on such ceremonial proceedings while meeting the Emperor.

Notwithstanding that, the Chinese Government never abandoned the pretense that foreign ministers should not put their petitions directly into the hands of the Emperor, so that we had resigned ourselves to put them into the hands of Prince Qing, who then approached the throne by the lateral stairs, threw himself down, and handed them over to the Emperor. Then he picked up the answer, which he then proceeded to read out to the visiting foreigners.

After my three bows, which the Emperor took for three *kowtows*, I read out my letter and while Prince Qing was getting closer to me to get them, I watched the Emperor and because of my height, I thought that I could leave them on the Emperor's desk myself. Since this would have constituted a precedent, I thought it was worthwhile to give it a try, so I advanced slightly and lifted them over the table.

---

49. The Guangxu Emperor (1871-1908) was the eleventh emperor of the Qing dynasty. His reign lasted from 1875 to 1908 but at that time the real ruler was his aunt Empress Dowager Cixi (1835 -1908). The Guanxu Emperor initiated the *Hundred Days' Reform* but it was abruptly terminated by a coup launched by the Empress Dowager in 1898, after which he was put under arrest in a palace at the centre of a lake until his death, which happened the day before the passing of Cixi. His reign title of Guangxu means *Glorious Succession*.

The Emperor appeared at that moment (he was about two meters away) to be of a youthful complexion, of yellowish skin but very pale, with a long face, a bit rachitic, with the lower lip slightly prominent, impassive but with expressive eyes, intelligent, I should say, curious and perhaps amazed by that change of protocol, finding it funny, because of my height that such new thing had been done. Encouraged by his faint smile, which seemed to me to appear on his face, I lifted slightly on my feet, extending my arm and pushing the letters from my King towards the Emperor who was clearly smiling by now, and who took the letters.

There was a pause in the automatic movements made by Prince Qing, who then proceeded to the throne and kneeled. The Emperor, putting the royal letters in front of him, took his answer out from his sleeve, and then passed it to the Prince, who came forward to read it. After one more bow, we withdrew, leaving by the same way and returning to the Legation. Vitale, after a few years in Beijing, was quite Sinicized and seemed very impressed by the new protocol; he discussed the matter with his foreign colleagues and, because of that, some of my colleagues came to ask me for more details of that news, which seems ridiculous today, but at that

The Italian legation in Peking, before the Siege

time, in Beijing, assumed some importance.

The next day Prince Qing came with two Ministers to protest that what I had done was irregular and could not be taken as a precedent to be used in the future. I answered that I had indeed ignored what had been done previously on similar occasions but on my side, I could not accept that I should have behaved in a different manner, and whenever I would be called upon to deliver letters from His Majesty the King of Italy I would hand them over in the same way, directly, or I would keep them with me.

I found some changes in the diplomatic corps in Beijing. The MacDonalds were on leave but they would return in the Autumn. A *Chargé d'Affaires* had taken MacDonald's place, he was an unpleasant man called Bax[50], who then left as soon as the Minister returned to his residence.

At the German Legation, von Heyking had departed, and Baron Ketteler[51] took his place, a rough German, who had previously been an interpreter at the Legation. His wife was a beautiful and likeable American. Acting as his secretary, an old acquaintance from Cairo had arrived: Below[52], a tall German, mellifluous but of a very good character, easy to get along with, learned and addicted to music. Then the *attaché* was a youth, Bergen[53]who, I believe, as I write, is Germany's Ambassador to the Vatican. But he never contacted me in Rome, and I don't miss him because I knew him little in Beijing and I have no sympathy nor desire to see again those who had *moved from the Monarchy to the Republic.*

---

50. Sir Henry George Outram Bax-Ironside (1859-1929).

51. Baron Clemens von Ketteler (1853-20 June 1900). His American wife was Maud Ledyard von Ketteler (1871-1960), from Detroit and daughter of Henry Ledyard, president of the Michigan Central Railroad.

52. Claus von Below-Saleske (1866-1939).

53. Carl-Ludwig Diego von Bergen (1872-1944).

At the Legation of France, there was Stephen Pichon[54], who had arrived during my first mission, and I should describe him now, because I forgot to mention him previously.

He was a Frenchman belonging to the lowest middle-class. It was said that he had worked in a typography position while young, as a printer, composing words on the galley. He was a militant of the extreme left and this had helped him greatly to improve his status. Elected to the chamber of deputies he had delivered a famous speech extolling the virtues of the *Commune*. That is what they said of him and he was accepted by us without great enthusiasm. But soon after we could see the good points of his character and we ended up liking him. He was a good devil, and not devoid of intelligence: perhaps not an eminent man but a good character, easy to get along with, very honest, loyal and open, therefore no *ficelle* (not vulgar) and, all in all, a good colleague. Ugly, not distinguished, not well educated; not really a man of the world but he tried to get along with all of us in the best possible way. Madam Pichon shared the same qualities of her husband and it was said that she was the daughter of the director of the *Maison Dorée*, the famous restaurant. In fact, Groovener used to say:"Quelle avait de la dame au comptoir." They kept us very entertained the first time they came to the Mass, on the first Sunday after their arrival. We were curious to see how they would behave: the wife was a Protestant and because of Pichon's political affiliation, that was the first time for both. On their special bench, they had an embarrassed air. Pichon was desperately looking left and right to observe our behavior and I, sitting close to the altar, in a fit of badness feigned a genuflection while the Gospel was read out, and they follow it, kneeling, while sitting down during the Elevation and so on. It was an impolite act on

---

54. Stéphen-Jean-Marie Pichon (1857-1933). He went on to have a brilliant career, becoming French Foreign Affairs Minister from 1906 until 1911.

my side, which I did when I was not close to them and I felt sorry after I came to know them, because that made them an object of fun, or better say, an object of smiles.

Shortly after my arrival, Pichon had fallen from his horse, breaking his nose and this certainly did not improve his looks. The longer he lived among us, the less his old sympathy for the communists' cause emerged in his conversation. During the stay of Prince Henry, the good Pichon who was sitting at the same table, forgot his old passion and told me that the political function of the British aristocracy was magnifying their merits; when I pointed out that in our countries that institution appeared diminished by an excessive interest in vulgar gossip he interrupted me and said: "Croyez, cher ami, que les intrigues de la court valaient mieux des intrigues de la basse cour qui nous avont maintenant." I looked at him in wonder and he, understanding the reason, added: "Ne vous étonnez pas de ce que je dis, mais on vielissant on met beaucoup d'eau dans son vin."

I had to admit that in the home of the Heykings there was very good wine and Pichon had mixed it with water. But such was his mentality. I believe that in Parliament he would had been the same; if he found himself in his old lodge, he would have returned to the old Pichon of his youth, but in Beijing there was no Parliament and there were no lodges.

The Austrian delegation had settled during my first residency, but I failed to mention the representative there, Baron Czikann,[55] a very tall gentleman. He was good, extremely correct, ignorant, a good colleague: he was taking care of the construction of his Legation and he owned a collection of *horns of his ancestors* as he himself said, in good faith. These were the horns of deer killed *by his ancestors*; he had taken them to Beijing, never failing to show them to all

---

55. Moritz Czikann von Wahlborn (1847–1909)

visitors when they went for lunch at his residence.

The tall Cologan was walking from a legation to the other. Solivares had told me that during the Spanish-American war he had written a letter to the Spanish Government, offering his arm for his Country. He was 67 and nearly blind! Perhaps his act of patriotism attracted attention and caused his recalling. He had been replaced by an original character, not devoid of intelligence, Anton de Olmet,[56] a brown Spaniard with a wavy black beard and curly hair. There were rumors swirling around that, during my absence, there had been friction between him and a colleague, caused by a woman: perhaps this was the reason why he had been recalled, with Cologan taking care himself of the limited work of the chancery.

In October, Caetani joined me soon after my family had joined me. During the winter the usual life went on with small dinners, tennis, and horse racing. Horse racing, fortunately, was very popular. I say *fortunately* because each of us kept several horses and because of this, during the Siege we always had horse meat to eat. From Mongolia, in the Autumn, we received many horses which were hairy, like little bears: we were buying them for one hundred Mexican dollars each, then we trained them, discarding the slowest ones. We had six or seven racing horses with which we were winning trophies, which the colleagues had put up, while they were winning those I had put up. I had thus six trophies in my apartment which were taken by the Boxers later, and I think I had put up six for my colleagues.

The Summer of 1900 had begun. The first rains were expected, dispersing the diplomatic corps to the Temples and the beach of Beidaihe, but it was then that troubles began, which forced us to stay locked inside the Legations from the

---

56. Fernando de Antón del Olmet y López de Haro (1872-1955).

12 of June until the 14 of August of that year.

Within the Legations there were slight differences on how to assess the first brawls which later degenerated into the Siege. Ketteler was a pessimist; he was insisting that a strong objection should be made to the Chinese Government to destroy the rebels and repel the Boxers who were approaching the Capital. Pichon was also very impressed by the progress of the disturbances and this was well before we came to fear for our personal safety.

Sir Claude agreed without resistance to the proposal of a common action, but he looked less pessimistic, which is somehow normal in a British man. He was rather worried that behind the pessimism of Ketteler there was some political scheming: "Vou savez, ces Allemands complottent toujours", he confided.

M. de Giers[57]was initially somewhat optimistic, if mysteriously so, but at the beginning refused to associate with our earlier proposals for a common action, then joined us after suggesting that we water down the form and thus the efficacy of our protests.

What he wanted to do, we did not know but we had the impression that he was working on something. We got a confirmation of this after having seen proof that he had secretly met, during the night, some emissaries of the Yamen, after we had agreed to leave aside all the private matters of our Legations, except questions of public order and not receiving Chinese privately but always with colleagues, and after having consulted with them. Even Pichon agreed that the conduct of his Russian friend was enough to justify doubts.

Joostens[58] arrived then and was unaware of what was happening. Cologan was the doyen of the diplomatic corps,

---

57. Michelle N. de Giers, Russian Minister. In Beijing 1897-1901.

58. Maurice Joostens (1862 – 1910). Minister of Belgium.

therefore he presided over our meetings and agreed with all of us; certainly, he was not *plotting* and no one among us had any doubt about the innocence of his actions. The Japanese representative stayed silent, smiled, and we left him a bit alone but, to tell the truth, I don't know why...

VI

The massacres of local Christians, and of some of the missionaries in the provinces, had been going on for a long time. They were the work of a faction or a sect, one of the many at work in China since immemorial times.

We were laughing at the beginning of the actions of the Boxers. I remember an evening when I, Below and Caetani, went to a certain small square following the narrow alleys of the Tartar city where, they told us, the members of a new sect were gathering to perform their ritual actions: we went, and we saw there some youngsters with red bandages around their legs and their arms, but they did not perform ceremonies or anything else, perhaps because we were watching, and our expedition ended in disappointment.

The most pessimistic at the beginning was an old missionary, father D'Addosio[59]. Tall, strong, with a long white beard, this old Neapolitan had an imposing appearance and the low voice of a bass singer, all things which gave him a very solemn air. He was kind to all the members of the Italian Legation and he had never made any political remark, but several hints made us think that he had an 'Italian' spirit. I was visiting him from time to time and he looked pained by the decree of the Empress with which she had granted a sort of worldly authority to the Catholic missions, promoting the Catholic bishop to a high level in the Chinese hierarchy. He though it to be a sort of bait, a trick played on Mons. Favier[60]. Father D'Addosio distrusted

---

59. Pasquale d'Addosio (1835-1900). He was a Vincentian priest (the order founded by St. Vincent de Paul) and he was from Lecce, not Naples as Salvago Raggi thought.

60. Pierre-Marie-Alphonse Favier-Duperron (1837-1905). Lazarite Vicar Apostolic of Northern Chi-Li and titular bishop of Pentacomia. He took part in the looting of Beijing.

Madam Pichon

the Empress and was sorry to hear of the praise given to her by Favier in France, after that decree magnifying the protection offered by France to the Church.

"That woman does not protect the flock, but she caresses the pastor", the missionary kept on repeating with a solemn tone.

When the Boxers started their activity, I noticed that Fr. D'Addosio was very impressed. He had assumed a prophetic tone and, new Jeremiah, was lamenting the fate of the Christians in China, a fate which he expected to be catastrophic. When the conditions in the city went from bad to worst and the actions of the Boxers raised alarm, we discussed among the diplomatic corps - after the murder of a British family – that it was better to inform the few Europeans remaining, for the greatest part Protestant missionaries dwelling outside the city walls, that as a prudent measure they should move inside the Legation quarter.

I thought about the Italians, like Father D'Addosio and a sister at the hospice outside the city where was the tomb of Father Matteo Ricci was located. Both belonged to the French Mission (Lazarists and the Sisters of Mercy) but there were Italians too, so I thought I had to take care of them. There were two more Italian sisters in Beijing, but these were lodged in the large mission at the Petang, a part of which was close to the Imperial Palace, therefore we thought that they were safer that the rest. Nevertheless, we thought that the Nantang was totally unsafe, as it was out of the city, located amid small Chinese buildings and little houses in a squalid quarter.

Unable to put our marines on horses and the distance being too great to ask them to follow on foot, we went alone with the *mafoo*, Caetani and I, departing early in the morning in the direction of the place where nuns of the mission lived close to the cemetery.

There were only two European nuns: the French superior

and an Italian, a likeable lady, not beautiful, but with sweet eyes. Both were impressed by the behavior of the population: in the evening a large crowd assembled in front of their gates, which led to their walled enclosure, shouting menacingly all night. With the morning, calm returned but even the superior was afraid that one night the gate would be breached. I remarked that two European ladies, living alone, should not be left in that situation and the superior, while agreeing with me, said: "Dieu veuille qu'on nous rappelle bientôt au Petang!". I spoke to the Italian sister, asking if she wanted to come to the Legation of Italy. There was a place for an Italian. She looked at me with gratitude in silence, but the superior said: "Notre devoire est de faire ce que nos superiours nous ordonnent. Le bon Dieu vous récompensera pour vos bonnes intentions mais ma soeur restera bien sure à sa place". The Italian nun agreed, with tears in her eyes, and while Caetani was talking to the superior, strolling in the garden, I remained with the Italian who told me that she was already resigned to the fact that she would die, but she was terrorized by the prospect of falling alive into their hands... and burst into tears, murmuring: *Ah, to possess at least a gun for having the illusion of defending...* I was truly disturbed by the desperation of that poor girl and I thought that Caetani had with him a small revolver; perhaps, he would agree to leave it to her. Then, at a certain shop in Legation street, he could buy a new one. I went close to Caetani and I whispered the proposal. He agreed and remained behind with the Italian sister, while I was walking with the Superior. But she noticed the revolver handed to the sister and smilingly told her: "Les messieurs son bien bons mais vous ne pouvez pas accepter qu'ils se privent de leur arme. Du reste vous le savez, ma soeur, nos armes à nous, c'est la prière. Rendez le pistolet, remerciez Mr. le Ministre et dites lui que la volonté de Dieu ser faite aver ou sans le pistolet". The nun returned the revolver, smiling through the tears and I must confess that I was moved by the dignity and strength of one, as well as by the discipline of the other, in spite of the horror they were expecting.

On the way out of the compound, I made up my mind to go to Mons. Favier, to tell him what I thought about the decision to leave two women alone among those brutes. The Monsignor was oscillating between the fear inspired by his years-long experience among the Chinese and hope because of the recent favors bestowed on him by the Empress. One time he looked certain that our worry for the future of the Missions was justified but then he looked calm and free from worries. I received a very unfavorable impression about him and before getting back I wanted to speak to Fr. D'Addosio. We found him, the only European in the Nantang and he seemed moved by my visit; as if I had run great risks going to him and he could not believe that save a few shouts, perhaps offensive, we risked nothing else. He nearly hugged me when I offered protection within the Legation, but he refused, saying that: "For more than thirty years I had taught to the faithful that for the sake of the religion one must be ready to give up his life; perhaps the time to confirm the facts in the sermons I had delivered had come and, besides that, I would have betrayed my ministry by abandoning my flock". And then he went on to say: "Do you believe that the Legations will be so secure? First will be us of the Missions, then the Legations. God wants to test this poor Country! Catastrophe is imminent!"

Having told him that I had been to see Mons. Favier, he stopped me, saying: "Oh, that wretched man! The demon of vanity has taken hold of him. I told him! I love him, he is an old friend of thirty years and I cry about his destiny. I wish him not to survive the pain, the remorse of not having opened the eyes of the Minister but to have succumbed to the praises of that unfortunate woman, an agent of Satan, who seduced him using his vanity. Poor Favier!" Then he insisted that I made haste to the Legation, he thanked me for having thought about him and he said that he would pray for us, for my family, and *for those sailors who had come here to die doing their duty. May God bless them all!*

Getting back home we concluded that the old man had been softened by age... but both Caetani and I were shaken and impressed by his serene, albeit catastrophic, prophetic spirit.

The next day Mons. Favier was at the French Legation to ask for sailors for the defense of the Peitang, the main Roman Catholic Cathedral, and then he came to me to complain about Pichon because he wanted to send only thirty soldiers, demanding that I also send some.

Since I thought that it was important to defend the Missions, I considered it proper not to refuse and so I wrote a card to Pichon stating that, if the Petang was an Italian Mission I would have already dispatched some sailors, but being a French Mission, I was not willing to give way to the insistence of Mons. Favier, unless he wanted me to send some. I gave the card to the Bishop, who went to Pichon and came back with his letter, in which he thanked me and begged me to send some Italian marines. Favier expressed his gratitude with tears in his eyes... and I pray that God may forgive his ingratitude towards the young sailors who died defending his Mission! Of the eleven men I dispatched, (if I remember well), six were killed.

After the Siege, Favier published a diary in which he made only a slight mention of *some Italians* at the defense of the Petang. He had not the moral courage to write that his Mission was saved because of the Italian marines. I reproached him in front of other prelates for that and he did not answer. Then I stood up and I left without saluting him. I have not seen him since.

On the 10th of June (if I remember well), rumors spread that more detachments of sailors and troops of different countries had left Tianjin, days before and were on the way to Beijing, commanded by the British Admiral Edward Seymour. The railway had been sabotaged but, they said, Admiral Seymour had abandoned the train and was proceeding on foot, following the rail lines and, having found an engine with few coaches, he was expected in the morning. This was the communication sent in a telegram... which was then interrupted by the cutting of the wires.

Understanding that the troops, not well organized for the march, would reach the station with difficulty and then had no way to transport ammunitions and equipment to the Legation quarter - the station was out of the city, a two hours' distance from our quarter - I collected some carts and I moved with Caetani and the *mafoo* to the station. I intended to facilitate the march of the Sirianni's detachment, part of the Seymour column, from the station to the Legation. We had several disturbances since, in the city, the Boxers were numerous and their effrontery was increasingly noticeable everywhere, especially against Europeans. There had also been some evident hesitation within the Legations about deciding if it was prudent to dispatch some Europeans to welcome the Seymour's detachment.

In fact, the only Europeans from the Legations present at the station were Caetani and I, in the company of four marines. When we arrived, we met two or three employees of the railway, many Chinese and local Chinese personnel of the Legations and one Japanese chancellor[61]. He had come, like us, with some carts to load their luggage.

Around the station, Chinese troops were camping and a General had transformed the waiting room into his headquarters. There was no precise news of the Seymour expedition. At around eleven o'clock a Chinese inspector arrived following the rails and he told the station master that

---

61. Akira Sugiyama was murdered that day, on the 11 June 1900 by the troops of the Muslim General Dong Fuxiang (1839–1908).

the European troops had stopped at about 20 kilometers from the station where the line had been interrupted. I thought about using one of the three engines laid idle in the station and an American engineer offered to drive it. We put together four wagons to be attached to the engine, but it seemed to me that the zeal of the engineer dropped when everything was ready. He said that, having no stoker, he could not depart. Having found among my four marines one who was a stoker, he volunteered to help and was accepted, but then the American declared the engine to be out of order. The station headmaster murmured that the American was drunk.

In the meanwhile, time was passing: neither the marines nor I had eaten breakfast and, of the Seymour expedition, we had no news: we did not know if they had camped, if they were carrying on, or if they would arrive later, during the night or not. I thought about getting back, so I instructed the marines to get on to a cart, and I left behind the other Chinese personnel with a letter for Lieut. Sirianni, then I departed.[62]

While I was in the process of departing, the Japanese chancellor came to me and asked what I had decided to do; on knowing my intentions, he told me that he had received orders from his Minister to wait for the Japanese detachment, so he would remain a little longer, and he asked me to inform his Legation about the reason for his delay; if he could not get further news of their detachment, then he would also head home.

On the way back, we noticed that the Chinese soldiers were assembled along the road which we were going to take, and that the attitude of their officers seemed quite hostile: they looked at us malevolently and we noticed that they made

---

62. Admiral Edward Seymour (1840-1929) had left Tianjin with 2.100 men on June 10. They had to fight large units of Boxers but, on the 16, they decided to turn back. At the Legation they nicknamed him *Admiral See-no-more.*

some menacing gestures. We increased the speed of our cart, in which we were with our four marines. At a certain point, due to some shouts from the officers, our *mafoo* turned to the field and we followed him, while getting up the road, further down. We reached the legation at around two. Passing in front of the Japanese Legation I saw a secretary and I told him about their Chancellor. At around three o'clock a Chinese servant employed by the Japanese Legation came back very agitated and told us that the Chancellor had waited until one o'clock and that while he was returning on his cart, the Chinese soldiers had stopped him, had pulled him out of the cart, and killed him.

We had probably passed before the order of attack had been given, or we were saved by the sudden detour taken by the *mafoo*.

The dash to the station made that morning by Caetani and I was later widely commented on in both a positive and a negative way. According to the first we had shown a lot of courage, while for others we had done something useless and foolish. All these comments, as is often the case, were equally exaggerated.

We had not shown a great courage, because, despite the situation, we were thinking that two armed Europeans on horses would be not attacked. In fact, until that day, when the Boxers were facing armed Europeans, they had always withdrawn as soon as the first shots from revolvers and rifles were fired. We were convinced that regular soldiers would not turn against us and therefore we were assured of the fact that we would face no danger at all, nor had we previously experienced great dangers.

My going there was not without merit, because if our detachment had arrived from Tianjin, made up of a few marines, without an interpreter and without means of transport, then they would have found them in a bad predicament. Therefore, I judged that my presence there was important, convincing the locals at the station to remain in their place and I thought that it was my duty to do it, even if it involved a certain degree of danger.

IL MANDARINO ZANONI VOLPICELLI.
(Da una fotografia di Afong, di Hong-Kong)

Eugenio Zanoni Volpicelli, Italian Consul in Hong Kong and Macau from
1899 to 1919

Camilla Salvago Raggi Pallavicino

VII

Completely isolated from the civilized world, while we were receiving news of massacres in the provinces, and with the members of a British family outside Beijing tortured and killed by the Boxers, we decided to go to the Yamen to persuade the Chinese Government to re-establish public order and safety, but then there was a small dissent among us. The minister of Germany wanted to announce our visit for the following day at nine o'clock, without waiting for their answer. Another thought it better to wait for their answer, to be certain that, at the right time, we would meet all of the Chinese ministers at the Yamen. We thought that we all agreed on this point. But Ketteler thought instead that we had all agreed to his proposal, therefore, while our letters to the Yamen requested a favorable reply to arrange for our visit, the letter of Ketteler announced his visit at the Yamen for nine o'clock sharp the next morning. The misunderstanding would cost Ketteler his life but saved ours.

In the morning, not having received an answer, we met Ketteler at the French Legation and the German representative, in accordance with what he had written, wanted to go, whereas we, equally insistent on what we had requested, were loath to go, because the risk was that once there we would not find any of the ministers. At that time, I believe, no one thought that going to the Yamen would entail mortal danger.

Our conclusion was that Ketteler should go; if he found the ministers on his arrival, then he would remain there and if he had not returned after half an hour, then we would follow in his footsteps, because that would have meant that he had found the Chinese ministers. I stayed on for a few minutes, talking to Pichon, and then I returned to my Legation, where I asked for my sedan chair to be prepared and then, shortly before the time we had set for the departure, I set out to see if Ketteler was returning. Instead of Ketteler, I saw the *mafoo* working at the German Legation and on seeing me he shouted *Tajen tokta.*[63] Thinking that I may have misunderstood I asked Rosthorn,[64] the interpreter and *chargé d'affaires* at the Austrian Legation what that man was saying and this was how I received the confirmation of the murder of my German colleague. I thought that an attack on the Legations by the Boxers was imminent and, therefore, I ordered the road to be closed and barricaded, and I put some of our marines on guard, ready to stop any aggression. Then I moved to the French Legation where Rosthorn had carried the sad news and where all the ministers met once more.

We may say that from that instant the Siege of the Legations began, because from that day we were unable to get out of our quarters, which we surrounded with barricades using the walls of the courtyards, pieces of stones taken from burned down and ruined buildings, and then we loaded on top some wooden beams and sacks full of earth. I believe that the work of preparing sacks to be filled with earth, which had fallen on the ladies, is partially responsible for their commendable behavior kept throughout the Siege. Since they were so busy all day, they had no time to feel scared.

The commanders of the *Legations' escorts* - such was the name we gave to the marines - had a meeting to decide how best to defend the Legations quarter and they had decided that all the provision of food and ammunitions should be kept at the British Legation, the easiest to defend, the largest, and where more easily all women and children would have found refuge when the space to defend had shrunk. It was thus decided that in case of a Chinese attack all family

---

63. In pidgin German that meant *Daren Tod!* That is: *the master is dead.*

64. Arthur von Rosthorn (1862-1945); his wife was Paula von Rosthorn (1873-1967).

members should move into the British Legation.

The reunion of the various families at the British Legation began, if I remember well, on the 18th of June, when the Belgian Minister Joostens with his secretary, Marqueling, abandoned their legation, because it was isolated from all the others, surrounded by Chinese huts and outside the Legation quarters. In the following days, the refugees seeking shelter in the British Legation increased in number and on the 21 June, I moved my family there, because the bullets were whistling over us, and it was not prudent to keep a lady, a chambermaid and a boy in that situation. I then returned immediately to my Legation, which I thought I was not going to evacuate because we were still hoping that the Chinese Government, for a certain time, would give a free rein to the Boxers but the arrival of a strong European contingent, which we thought imminent, would help to clear the mind of the Empress and her advisers. We soon came to realize that the Chinese soldiers had joined the Boxers. Such optimism on our side had shocked many of the usual critics, those who had never been to China or who visited China after the events. They questioned our knowledge of the real situation: they claimed that while living among the Chinese we had understood nothing and as career diplomats we should have known the Chinese' mood, but we had been unable to forecast anything. To criticize is easy, but we, the diplomats, were not the only ones who had failed to see this storm gathering.

During the first days of June, the first or the second if I remember well, the family of Sir Claude was still on the hills outside the city and the British Minister, planning to send them to Japan, consulted Sir Robert Hart, a China resident for forty years and head of the Chinese administration, thought to be the greatest expert on that society. His written answer is on record, and one can read the following sentence: "I am convinced that in the Empire some grave disorders will happen, but the safest city of all China will certainly be Beijing, and the most secure place in Beijing will be the Legations quarter."

Less than fifteen days later I saw Sir Robert Hart entering the French Legation, carrying a small suitcase. His home, adjoining the Legation, was in flame and sacked, while rifle shots were heard within the Legations quarter.[65]

The assailants tried to burn our home, throwing petrol with an anti-fire engine taken, I believe, from the Custom house, and then they fired rockets. We had to stay on the rooves to extinguish the fire and some of the marines were slightly wounded, because the Chinese were firing at us while we were over there.

The Legations quarter was divided by a canal: on the right the Legations of Great Britain, Russia, the United States and Holland – therefore the British, Russian and American detachments were assigned the task to defend the north-west of the west side and the south-west corners. On the left bank were the other Legations, and the detachments of France and Japan were given the northern corner, to the Austrians, the north-east, to the Italians the east and to the Germans the south-east; the south was defended by the wall placed between the Tartar and the Chinese city, nine meters high and at least six meters wide.

Bad luck dictated that in Beijing an Austrian navy captain, Edward von Thomann had the highest rank among the army officers. Being superior in degree, he took control of various detachments on the left bank (Japan, France, Austria, Italy, and Germany).

In the early morning of the 22nd there was a strong attack against the Italian Legation with vicious fire coming from

---

65. Camilla Salvago Raggi Pallavicino writes: "Those good China experts were never able to guess right about anything…also about the Hanlin library. On the 23 June at 11 in the morning the Chinese burned it down in the hope that the strong northerly wind would burn the Legations." The experts were sure that the Chinese would have spared their great library.

some small huts to the east. From the barricade we had placed on the road Paolini[66] decided to make a dash in that direction, which he did together with Caetani, while I remained on the street together with the marines. At that time, from the house facing the Legation, where the tutor of the Emperor had lived, they began to shoot arrows aimed at our backs: some hit the walls and there remained embedded. We were not hit and it was enough to send some marines who, after breaking down the door, entering the garden and fired a few shots, to see those archers flee. While Paolini, Caetani and a few marines were returning to the barricade, happy to have dislodged the enemy from the huts, we received an order from Edward von Thomann to retreat. We were surprised: Paolini refused to withdraw, and I went to the Austrian commander. I found him in front of the Austrian Legation, busy arranging for the retreat of a column of French and Austrian soldiers, ready to cross the canal to reach the British Legation. I tried to convince him to stop that maneuver but he, very excitedly, told me that the Chinese had penetrated the space between us and the British legation, and had already taken the bridge, therefore we had to counterattack, breaking through their ranks to reach our allies in order not be cut off from them. I demanded an explanation for that incredible news, and he started to shout with his characteristic Italian: "Quel ufficiale italiano ubbidisca al suo superiore! Venga subito!"[67]. In the meantime, the Japanese and German detachments were joining the other two and moved toward the bridge in a very bad mood. It was then that we became resigned to the fact that we would need to withdraw, and I thought that we would have to fight to reach the British Legation.

---

66. Lieutenant Tommaso Federico Paolini (1873 – 1926). Decorated with a gold medal for his actions in Beijing. During the war between Italy and Turkey (1911 - 1912) he commanded the submarine Argo and during WWI he was in command of several naval units.

67. That Italian officer must obey his superior. He should come immediately!

Instead, we reached it without seeing a single Chinese. I ran to the place of Sir Claude, where I found also Pichon and Giers. They all believed that we had been repelled by the Chinese, and, on learning how things were, Sir Claude exclaimed: "If we follow this way our end is close!"

I answered that we should get rid of commander von Thomann[68] and to remedy the situation, the only solution would be to give the general command to Sir Claude, who had been in the army. All agreed. Sir Claude accepted on condition that we would give him a written note. I took a pen, I wrote, and I asked to Pichon and Giers to sign. The British Minister read it, stood up and said: "Salvago, take the Italian, French and German detachments and go to retake the Legations."

Twenty minutes later the Japanese and the Germans retook their Legations without firing a shot: the French and Italians were engaging the Chinese who had occupied half of the French Legation. Our Legation had been burned down. We repelled the Chinese, pushing them out of almost all of the French Legation. I returned to inform Sir Claude and to ask where to go with the Italian marines, having lost our Legation. Sir Claude indicated the Palace of Prince Su, between the Canal and the Japanese Legation. There we camped until the end of the Siege.

---

68. He was then hit by a shell and buried on the 8th of July.

VIII

Sir Claude MacDonald was perfect. He held the command with tact, moderation and wisdom. There was no need to display a great military skill but only to keep things under control and be careful. In doing so, Sir Claude was the perfect man. Calm, not wanting to show any theatrical heroism, he possessed the tranquility of a country squire.

I remember that he lost his patience only once with poor Marqueling, who was strutting around here and there without knowing what to do, armed to the teeth with two large revolvers inside his belt, plus a rifle and a bayonet on the side. A day in which Sir Claude stumbled on him two or three times and then he saw him again entering the hall, losing his cool he told me to send away that sort of *Calabrian brigand*. As soon as he said that, noticing my ironic smile, since it was incorrect to talk to me about Calabrian brigands, he realized his *gaffe* and told me: "Sorry, Salvago, today I am a bit irascible and I am saying silly things; send him away and keep in mind the fact that he had nothing to do with the Calabrese, some of whom are valiantly fighting at the Prince's palace."

Another day, after Livio Caetani had behaved very bravely in an accident which happened during the previous night, Sir Claude came to me at our barricade to congratulate him and he offered warm words of praise, unfortunately ending with the sentence: "I can see that you have British blood in your veins." Caetani darkened in the face and, as he was leaving, I told Sir Claude how unfortunate his words had been. At first, he did not realize his mistake, but then he understood, so he stepped back and, recalling Caetani, said to him: "I did not make myself clear, I wanted to say that after learning how you had behaved, I felt proud thinking that you have in your veins some British blood."

Once we were alone, again he told me: "Please, do not think that I am a *gaffeur*: it is simply that you ascribe certain meanings to my words, which are just not there, and thus it is necessary for me to explain things properly to avoid your sinister interpretations of my most innocent sentences."

Pichon was not made for that situation. Impressionable, good, he cried like a baby when one of his marines was killed and ended up looking ridiculous because his own soldiers were the first to laugh.

Poor Pichon, he made an effort to go all mornings to his Legation, among his marines, even if he could not hide the state of his nerves. All were afraid of being hit by a bullet, but they did not show their fear, while he was showing it: this was the only difference. Unfortunately, he had the habit of going around with a two-barrel hunting rifle on the sling to which he had cleverly fixed a large kitchen knife as a bayonet. This funny weapon was always with him!

One day, seeing me going to the Legation, he asked whether he could accompany me. We approached a bridge which we had to cross, a dangerous passage, because it was roofless, therefore it was not prudent to linger on it longer than necessary, and one had to cross quickly. Pichon crossed it too quickly... and seeing him overtaking me, short, fat and with that rifle... it was a funny sight, I was caught by a *fou rire* which made me stop. Once he had reached the cover he turned, looking furious, and he shouted back at me: "Voyon, venez vite, c'est idiot de rester là se ficher de moi!" Once back on the covered road we continued at normal speed, but unfortunately that scene was observed by some British soldiers and then the story went around...

On the evening of the 14th, things were going badly at the French Legation. Pichon had gone there in the morning, and then a mine had buried four or five French soldiers. The

Chinese took advantage of this to advance and, with some difficulties, they were stopped on a second line but there the French were not so strongly entrenched. Luckily, the Chinese did not take advantage of the favorable situation and at night, when I left, the French were fortifying the new line of defense. Our hope - which was realized - was that during the night the Chinese would remain quiet, letting us improve that line. On returning to the British legation I went to see Pichon in his room, while he was having dinner with his wife and she was trying to console him while he kept his head in his hands, crying. I entered and I reported to him how the situation was and he lifted his head, looked at his wife and exclaimed: "Je te l'ai dit, ma chère, nous sommes foutus". The lady was trying to calm him down with several: "Voyons mon ami..." But he was insisting and repeated: "Foutus, je te dis, foutus!" so much so that at the end I told his wife: "Madame, dites-lui que nous sommes foutus, ou il se fache!" and my joke was a useful diversion, because instead of crying he jumped and I had to run, while he hurled insults at me. The next day, Pichon came to see if I was offended, and he apologized, blaming his weak nerves: "Je le sais bien que je n'ai pas les nerfs pour ça!" concluding: "Mais je n'ai pas pris la carrière militaire, je me suis fait diplomate! Est-ce que je-pouvais penser qu'un diplomate devait aussi faire le métier?". After all he was right, and I should add that during our discussions he always behaved well, with calm, more reasonably than others and not at all timidly.

Of Giers, the Russian Minister, one could not really say that he had not *une bonne presse*. In the Spring, when we found that he had not been *very loyal* and was seeing Chinese officials without informing us, although he had promised not to do so, all were saying that he was *betraying us*. This was the rumor which had spread among the civilians; this was how we referred to all those who were not part of the Legations but were quartered in the two *tingers*. They had been, for the greatest part, employed by the railway, including a few shop keepers and foremen. Several Belgian, French, one or two Germans; I don't think there were British among them. The sinister rumor (about Giers' double play) had spread and one day Giers refused to come to meet MacDonald because he needed to cross the *tingers* and he could not tolerate the unfavorable comments which were meted out in passing. After that, I had to accompany him, having "negotiated" our passage with their managers.

There was some exaggeration in that rumor, but Russian policy before the Siege was not a pleasant one because they tended to let things get worse, to oppose a Japanese intervention and finally let their army intervene and squash the disturbances, even if their troops crossing the Amur could come only after several months... They would have thus intervened to *vindicate* us, while our desire was that somebody would come *earlier*, with no need to vindicate us.

Furthermore, Giers was not a pleasant person because, on looking at him, we all got the impression of falsity and duplicity. I believe that this was an accurate representation of his character.

Lady Giers was a good woman and she spent most of her time indoors, but they had a daughter, around twenty years old, who was like a bad accident: ugly and slightly malignant.

One day I stumbled, close to the tennis court, into poor Ms. X. She was the gracious wife of a young British interpreter who had a one-year-old daughter. She was bitterly weeping because her daughter was starving to death. There were no milk and eggs. She asked me if I would accompany her to the young Miss Giers, whom she did not know, to ask if by chance she an egg to spare, since the Giers had two chickens. We explained the predicament to the young Miss Giers who told us that she had three eggs and she could spare one for us: but first she wanted to know what she could get in return. The poor mother seemed to revive on knowing that she had found an egg to save her daughter... at least for a day. She had some difficulty in understanding what the young lady wanted in return for her egg, but finally realized that she could get it if she was able to supply something in exchange, and then she started to list all the delicatessen items she could give her: a box of sardines, a bottle of Worcester sauce, or a bowl of *foie-gras*. At the mention of the sardines, the girl furrowed her nose, when hearing of the offer of sauce, she looked down, although her face brightened on hearing about the *foie-gras*. I was upset, and I said: "I now realize that to give an egg to this poor lady for her daughter is a sacrifice too great to make. I hope to spare you the trouble." I had remembered that Madam Pichon had two hens and so I took the girl to her. Indeed, she had eggs, and when the young mother asked her what she wanted in exchange, Madame Pichon was offended and answered: "La nouvelle que mes pauvres oeufs on fait du bien à votre petit me suffit". I confess that I repeated the story several times, and it certainly did not improve the *mauvaise presse* regarding that Russian girl.[69]

Cologan was the most pleasant man at the Siege. He contributed greatly to keep the morale high, even with the ladies, with his comic, pleasant and courageous behavior. He was taller than me, and skinnier, with a short beard, sparse, and grey. On his head, he wore a round sun cap which, we found, looked like the elm *of* Mambrinus, and in fact he looked like the *knight with the sad countenance*.[70]

---

69. Some Chinese civilians were able to conduct a small trade with the people inside the Legations and according to Camilla S.R. Pallavicino: "We organized small exchanges and we did manage to get some eggs. A Chinese took some eggs inside and our sailors bought one each, then sent them to me and my son. To listen to this while having a breakfast or lunch in our home is not so impressive but thinking about those poor young men who were living on horse meat and had little bread, I was moved by their action. After they insisted, I agreed to keep 4 for me and my son and the rest we sent to the wounded."

70. Mambrinus is a fictional Moorish character in chivalry romances. According to legend, he possessed a helmet of pure gold which rendered

Cologan had no marines and he did not know what to do, so he decided that his job was to entertain the ladies. A fire destroyed the Krulf warehouse (a Dane, who owned the only store of Beijing). On collapsing, the walls had covered the goods it contained so that several batches had not burned. Cologan often went to search among those ruins and then triumphantly offered to the ladies some soap and toothbrushes with dentifrice. It was a blessing for the ladies, who were unaware that bullets were often whistling close to Cologan, and since he was so tall it was not easy for him to duck and keep his head down. I pointed this out to him, but he answered that: "Yes, it is true I am a bit too tall... but on the other hand I am so thin that it will not be easy for them to hit me."

Cologan regularly became furious when talking of Knobel.[71] The Dutch Minister was still young, I believe he was forty or a little more; he was strong and robust but he was seized by a crazy fear, and he had locked himself up in a sort of cellar, the only place underground at the Legation, and he was not moving out of there: he had food delivered there and we never saw him. When, at a certain point, the Chinese were hoping to catch us in a trap, negotiating our departure, Cologan, who was the 'dean' among us, had to summon all the diplomats to read the letters sent by the Chinese and then decide what to answer. The meeting was arranged in MacDonald's studio; it was then, for the first time, that Knobel appeared, pale after so many days locked up in the cellar and a little thinner than before. On seeing him coming, Cologan, normally kind and good, felt his Castilian blood of a knight of the Mancia boil in his veins, and he stood up, extending his long arm, and shouted: "Allez vous-en, allez vous cacacher! Vous êtes la honte du corps diplomatique!"

---

its wearer invulnerable. Don Quixote found a barber's basin and insisted that it was the enchanted helmet of the Moorish King.

71. Frits Fridolin Marinus Knobel (1857-1933).

As it can be seen our nerves were a bit shaken. But the good thing was that the unlucky man went away without opening his mouth, and I did not see him again until the day after the arrival of the European troops. He was then on the walls, close to another gentleman, when a stray bullet, coming from I don't know where, superficially pierced his thigh. He fell, and he was taken into the Legation; the bullet had just penetrated a couple of centimeters below the skin and was removed. Knobel recovered for six or seven days on a *chaise-longue* in the garden. All those who reached Beijing then went to salute the heroic Minister, the only one wounded by enemy fire!

I don't think that the Knobel's case should be seen as a surprise. I believe that, in all wars, there are similar kinds of heroes, and I have noticed that in life similar cases do occur, even when bullets are not flying.

Joostens, the Belgian Minister, was still young but had heart disease, which was made worse by the Siege and killed him a few years later. He had come to Beijing a few weeks before the Siege and (an unlucky fact which he often deplored with sincere regret) had come with some caskets of excellent wines, which had been placed with care in a cellar, but then fell into Chinese' hands. He had received from Sir Claude a room at the British Legation to share with his secretary, Marqueling. This man - which one day MacDonald would call a Calabrian brigand - was the pain in the neck of the Minister, because before going to sleep he never missed an opportunity to deplore the fact that he had had to delay a holiday to Japan, otherwise: "I would not be living in such a jail", he mumbled before closing his eyes. Another affliction disturbed the day of poor Joostens. During the flight from his Legation he had not taken suits to change and the elegance of his *mise* suffered from the impossibility to change. His jacket, so well cut, was not looking good as it was covered with spots, and his shirt changed color every day, but these colors were moving far from the original white. Finally, Joostens found a piece of fabric and he tailored a sort of *plastron* which replaced the missing shirt. On all that he put on a brooch with a splendid pearl, which appeared rather incongruous, being the only remaining trace of an ancient elegance.

Below, the German *chargé d'affaires* remained in his Legation, protected to the south by the high walls of the Tartar city and on the north by the Legations of France and Japan. He had thus the commodity of a large house, having all his suits and shirts and - an important detail - a very famous cook. The local personnel had run away, if heathens, and remained if Christians; not because of affection towards the master of the house but in order not to be massacred. Our disgrace was that generally the cooks were mostly non-Christians and we had lost them; their flight, the scarcity of what was needed for good cooking (butter, milk, eggs) rendered barely eatable the two slices of horse meat daily granted to each of us.

Below had been lucky because the cook, although a heathen, had no time to flee and was carrying on with his duties, preparing dishes every day which, by the description he was giving us, created in us a lot of envy. Below was a melomaniac, and he spent part of his day playing the piano in his sitting room on the south side, which was out of the range of the Chinese bullets. His cook hated the bullets which were shot by his countrymen, but he loved music, and obtained permission from his master to take shelter there while the fighting was going on, therefore one could frequently be found playing the piano, while the other was trembling in a safe corner of the room. The fact that some bullets often whizzed into that room made Bulow unhappy and he exclaimed: "Quelles sales gens, les Chinois! Ils sont vraiment degoutants!" with the characteristic northern sign reserved to shoo away flies.

Conger,[72] the United States Minister, to look more warlike had put on the lapel of his jacket a small blue ribbon showing affiliation with I know not which unit, perhaps a shooting club, and was often congregating with his militarized missionaries, who pretended to be doing a lot of work in the defense of the Legations.

Among the civilians, a young German was prominent: he had been employed by a railway consortium and I think he was an officer of the reserve. He had collected twenty volunteers from different countries who formed a group of brave and valiant fighters. At the French Legation, Sabbione and Benvenuti were fighting alongside the French marines: they distinguished themselves and, when the Siege was over, Pichon managed to grant them the Legion D'Honneur.

During the Siege, I met Fr. D'Addosio, who was going around among his faithful camped at the Fu[73] of the Prince, indifferent to the bullets and looking even more like a biblical prophet than before.

Colonel Shita, the Japanese military attaché, was the most capable military man at the Siege. Small, round, planted on his two small legs a bit too short, he was always moving and smiling even when he was telling us of the conditions, which were not at all nice, and of the defense to which he contributed more than anybody else.

---

72. Edwin Hurd Conger (1843-1907) was a soldier, diplomat, lawyer, banker and an Iowa congressman.

73. *Fu* meant Palace or Park, a short form of *Su-wang-fu*.

Camilla Salvago Raggi, daughter of Paris Salvago Raggi, in 2014.

IX

We had tried to send some messengers to Tianjin. I believe we had sent about fifteen. They were Chinese, to whom we promised very high rewards if they came back with answers. We lowered them down from the outer walls of the Tartar city, towards the Chinese city. Then they had to get out of the Chinese city, reach Tianjin and get back with answers. I think that no more than three or four made the journey. One was captured by the Boxers, and he began a correspondence with us with the aim of letting us fall into a trap but, on the contrary, it helped us to gain some time and, contrary to their aims, was something that contributed to our salvation. One returned by the end of June with a letter from the Russian consul, in which he assured us that troops would come to our rescue *soon after the rainy season* that is, the end of September; this, because of the scarcity of food, was equal to a declaration of death and I extracted from Giers the promise that he would keep it secret, otherwise that would have pushed everybody to despair. In fact, he only informed Sir Claude and Pichon of it.

A Chinese boy, a student of the American missionaries, sent to Tianjin, managed to reach the city but he could not contact the Europeans for several days because he only spoke Chinese, and was repulsed by the Europeans he tried to speak to, who thought he was a beggar. At the end, he was lucky enough to meet an interpreter and being finally able to speak he passed our letters to him. Then, during the night of the first of August, if I remember well, a faint call heard near the wall told us that he was back.

The letters were carrying sad news. Troops had not departed. The British Consul (an old wimp) was *praying for us* and *at a lunch at the Consulate he had drunk to our health.*

Another messenger was sent informing them of our conditions to spur the troops forward, since hunger and lack of ammunitions were announcing our impending doom.

Even though we had reduced the rations of meat to two small pieces every day, and the bread (war bread with bran) to three small slices per day, we were left with few horses and little grain.

To save on ammunition, we were *fishing* during the night dead Chinese soldiers with bent nails attached to ropes, over the barricades, catching them by their belts: we then removed the bullet holders and threw back the bodies. Using this system, we also fished up several rifles. Such night fishing was very tiring, very disgusting, leading to limited results, but it did save us a lot of ammunition. When the troops liberated us, the Italian soldiers had just eleven bullets each for their rifles. A few days later another messenger announced that the troops would leave Tianjin at the beginning of August.

We thought then to let them get a clear indication of the Legation quarter, where we were barricaded, to avoid the danger of being bombarded. I reproduced on a thin paper a plan of the city, reduced in size to a page of a notebook, where I indicated the Petang and the Legations quarter. The map was sewn into the sole of the shoe of the boy who had already reached Tianjin and had then returned. After only three or four days we heard his call under the wall: he had already gone to and returned from Tianjin. We learned that, *en route* he had spotted some cavalry soldiers wearing black uniforms, with sabers; they gave him the chase and thinking himself lost, he knelt and made the sign of the cross. His luck was that one of the Indians (they were Indian cavalry), even though he was a Muslim, had been the attendant of a Christian officer, and when he saw him making the sign of the cross, he stopped his comrades. The intelligent lancer, seeing that small Chinese boy praying like his officer, thought that he should be taken back alive. Then the map of Beijing, which I had drawn, was handed to General Gaselee.

The messenger returned with two letters, one from the British General for Sir Claude and one from a Japanese General to Shita. Not having a cipher code, the former had simply written: "I am coming with a strong army after having twice defeated the enemies. Keep up the spirits".

The Japanese General had the cipher and he read that he was leaving Yangtseng, and they planned to reach, on the 12th, Tung Chiao and on the 14th, Beijing. I think that no message was more welcome than that.

Only at that moment, we began to think that we might come out alive from that situation. While we were reading, the children were playing at the "Boxers" in the hall. Sir Claude looked at me and said: "Perhaps those children will see Europe again." Although he was British, he looked a bit moved to me.

Poor Sir Claude, he was not feeling well at all. He had been suffering from dysentery for several days, and two days earlier, Doctor Pool had asked me to look after him and not let him get too tired, being very worried about his heart condition. I then tried to convince him that he should remain resting on the *chaise-longue* and send me around on urgent matters. Those days were terribly tiring for me because, besides the reappearance of old injuries from Spain and Russia, I had injured a leg and my knee had swollen after my fall from a roof.

It was raining heavily and the Chinese, having lost hope of snaring us into their trap, had started again to fire with their rifles and cannons, with even greater energy than before.

On the evening of the 13 of August, during the incessant fire from Chinese rifles, Sir Claude asked me to carry out a complete inspection of all barricades to recommend a more watchful care of them, while we were hoping for the speedy arrival of our troops.

Sir Claude's worry in those last days was that the

enthusiasm for the impending liberation would result in negligence in watching the barricades, thus causing our utter ruin.[74]

At around seven I was on the Italian barricade: Caetani was as calm as usual and it seemed that he did not realize that our chances of survival were by now very high, because he had never believed in it. The marines looked in good spirits. At the Japanese barricade I found Shita preoccupied by the same worry as MacDonald. He told me that he was keeping a watchful eye on the Austrians, his neighbors on the right, because after a certain accident which had happened in July, he did not trust their nerves.

The navy officer Darcy[75] was at his place, as usual energetic, indefatigable and sure of being a great strategist. He was really a man who knew his job and discharged it well. There was also Miss Rosthorn: so pleasant, brave, always full of good humor, contrary to the character of her husband. The bad character of her husband indirectly determined some circumstances which gave her a halo of sympathy, of being a little heroine, a fame in part justified but quite exaggerated.

During the first days of the Siege, Rosthorn, who was living in the British Legation with his wife, quarreled with Sir Claude about certain shovels and hoes which belonged to the Austrians but were seized by the British to carry out certain works. The quarrel grew, and then Rosthorn and his wife moved out of the British Legation. He requested and obtained hospitality at the French Legation, where Austrian marines were already serving. Therefore, she became the only lady remaining with the combatants. A thing which was materially true, even if the distance separating her rooms

---

74. Camilla S.R. Pallavicino: "Half an hour later from the corridor I heard somebody calling me, it was the Minister of Spain, the good Mister Cologan, who put himself in charge of giving all the good news: "Madame, Madame, nos troupes sont aux portes de la ville.."

75. Eugene Darcy (1861-1916).

from the line of fire was equivalent to the distance separating the rooms of several ladies in the British Legation from the line of fire. But she was alone in the Legation of France and then mixed with the soldiers, as there were no old people there or 'merchants. Therefore, she was more *at the front* than the other ladies. She had a lot of zest, a lot of courage and those officers loved that, it made them enthusiastic, and her fame as a heroine, greatly justified, was consolidated. It increased, of course, after the Siege.[76]

I met Bulow that evening, he was really nauseated by *des sales chinois*. They had started to hurl small grenades against his house and bit by bit were demolishing the south-east side of his Legation. If they carried on doing that, they would have rendered inhabitable his sitting room with the piano. He gave me a whisky with warm water, which I found revolting.

I went on top of the German barricade, with my very painful knee. Lieutenant von Saden, tall, thin, and rigid as a good German is, was always standing to attention and not willing to relax the discipline he was enforcing on his men. They were surprisingly well dressed, as they had remained in their barracks, but I suspected that they had some tin cans hidden away or taken from the Legation's stock because they looked better fed than our marines. I rested there a bit and then I crawled to the west barricade, the American one. They were nice looking boys but I don't know why they had the air of being more like cowboys than soldiers. I went down to the Russians and then I completed my tour at around nine o'clock: I was dead tired, and after giving my report to MacDonald I went to lie on my mattress, crossing a small antechamber where Japanese chambermaids, all naked, were merrily taking a bath in a tub, as if that was the most natural thing in the world. I was very sleepy, so much so that I did

---

76. Paula von Rosthorn (1873-1967). Lionized by the Press, known as 'Good Fairy of the Defence'. After the Siege she received the Order of Elizabeth and the Legion d'Honneur.

not notice my wife when she came to sleep in the same room where I was resting.

Suddenly I woke up. Further to the usual uproar made by the Chinese rifle fires the bangs of cannons were audible, quite different from the isolated Chinese ones. It was far away but… different. Our soldiers were coming!

The joy I felt is hard to describe but I was so tired that I had no desire to stand up and go to see and I just stayed there, listening to it, filled with beatitude.

Then, very far away, some machine gun bursts were fired, and they were also certainly ours. The sound was different compared to the Chinese ones and it was so clear that my wife, realizing that I was awake, asked if they were certainly ours this time. Then she told me to go to see and I understood that I had to stand up, so I put my jacket on and I went to the hall. There were several ladies there.

Sir Claude, who was anxious to see me, was still in bed but he was standing up and he told me that he knew I was very tired but he did ask me to go around the barricades again, because: "This" he said "Is the most dangerous time. It would be unforgivable to let those damned people inside! Listen how they are furiously shooting. They are doubling their rage and they do hope to finish us before the arrival of our soldiers. Go, and persuade all that we'll have to wait a long time before our troops will enter. Go and recommend them to hold on, to hold on for a few hours, let's just hold on!"

I departed once more at three in the morning. I repeated the tour of the previous evening. The Chinese's shooting was growing more intense but they did not move, they seemed to be preparing for an attack but they were not coming forward. Reaching the top of the walls with the light of the sunrise I could see the small clouds created by the shrapnel on the east wall of the Chinese and Tartar city. Never did a landscape looked more appealing than that to me! I sat on the ground with my back to the wall to get some rest and to ease my painful leg and… I fell asleep!

An American soldier woke me up at eight or nine in the morning, telling me that the sun on the head was dangerous. I went down, going back to see Sir Claude and then I went to the dining room to have my usual cup of tea and the usual piece of bread. A little bit later I was looking inside a door where there was a group of people composed of Doctor Pool, another officer and a very lurid man, covered with slime; I could not see if he was a Chinese or a European as he was covered in filth, and he seemed to have been rolling in it. I went closer and I saw some blond hairs and gray eyes. Pool presented to me, with British formality, Lieutenant X[77] who stood up to attention and, answering my caring questions, said that he had crawled under the barricade of the canal to precede his comrades. The barricade was going to be demolished and the general would enter shortly. I rushed to Sir Claude and we came out together; moving from the tennis court, we saw a group of officers advancing, one of whom looked aged and had a white mustache. Sir Claude moved toward him and asked: "General Gaselee?" The officer nodded and asked: "Sir Claude MacDonald?" They shook hands, perhaps a bit more warmly than if casually meeting on the road.[78] Very calmly, the General said that he was glad to have reached us on time. Sir Claude answered that he was glad that the first to arrive was a British General. Not a word more. The General looked around and asked if the intervention of his soldiers was urgent in certain places. Sir Claude turned to me and asked me to accompany him to the entrance of the Legation, where there was a barricade which was cutting the road to the Imperial city, right on the

---

77. Almost certainly Henry Bathurst Vaughan, Commander of the 7th Rajputs.

78. Camilla S.R. Raggi: "General Gasalee was a fine tall man, with a dark face covered with dust on which two white mustaches appeared prominently."

bank of the canal, where the fire from the Chinese was more intense. A young officer followed, commanding a group of fifty Indians. I accompany them to the designated place and the first Indian who put his nose into an embrasure fell with his head punched by a bullet. I returned and I found the General sitting on a step, close to Lady MacDonald.

Down at the tennis court the British ladies were drawing water from the well, pouring the buckets on the heads of some young officers who were covered by dust, who then thanked them and departed with their Indians to the north of the Legation. One hour later the Chinese had abandoned their side of the barricades and around the Legation there were no more enemies. I ran to the Italian trench at the Fu and I found nobody, I shouted, and no one answered. I lifted my hat on a stick and, not receiving the usual volley of bullets, I crossed and, with a lot of care, I walked through the Chinese encampment, where I saw some dead bodies but no living soul; I moved forward, towards the great road bordering the northern part of the Fu, and there I heard some shouts of *Avanti!* and rifle shots.

On the road, I saw Paolini with his left arm suspended to the neck, a revolver in his hand, running ahead of a dozen marines who were stopping to aim and shoot, chasing a group of Chinese escaping to the north in a cloud of dust. I did manage to reach them despite the state of my leg, and I convinced Paolini not to get lost with a dozen men within the narrow alleys of the city, where the Chinese hidden behind a house could liquidate *all the Italian forces*. Of the 28 Italian soldiers he had in June, he had lost seven and eight were recovering from their wounds at the hospital. The Siege was over.

Then I thought about the eleven Italian marines at the Petang, so I went to Pichon, and I asked him to take care of them. He came with me to MacDonald and in the evening, we were able to talk to General Gesalee. He declared that it was impossible to venture out during the night and get to the Petang but he promised to call me in the morning to let me know. Unfortunately, in the morning General Frey came. Pichon called me and we started to discuss our plans. We had to find a map of the city, and we explained to him how to get there and which way to follow. Major General Henry Frey wanted to get on the wall to see. I don't know what he wanted to see. Finally, he declared that he could not get there without cavalry *pou éclairer le chemin*. We returned, hoping to restart soon but the cavalry was promised for the next morning!

Once home I learned that Fr. D'Addosio had departed alone with his small donkey, followed by his Chinese sacristan.[79] One hour later his local adjutant came back saying that he had been captured by the Chinese. We came to know in the following days that he was taken to the Palace of Prince Tuan: there he was martyrized and thrown into a well.

Ten days later I ordered the Palace of Prince Tuan and all inside it, including his ancestors' tablets, to be burned to the ground. On the ruins, I put a proclamation written in Chinese that this had been done to vindicate the death of the Italian missionary. I don't know if that was the right thing to do but I do know that if I ever find myself in the same situation again then I would do the same. We should not judge things of the past using today's mentality.

On the next morning a battalion of infantry, French marines and a squadron of Indian cavalry directed by several volunteers who were pointing the way, went to the Petang.

____

79. Camilla S.R. Pallavicino: "On the 15 August in the morning the French soldiers wanted to depart but for reasons I don't know exactly they stopped. Father D'Addosio, who was already mounting a donkey, wanted to join them but on seeing them delay in liberating the mission, where some of his friends were still alive and starving, wanted to depart to tell them news of the liberation. He went alone, perhaps hoping to convince others to follow him, but his departure was ignored by most and half an hour later the news spread that he had been wounded."

I went with Caetani, taking six marines. We reached the gate through which, from the Tartar city, one enters into the Easter side of the Imperial palace. There a short Japanese captain came forward and speaking a French completely devoid of the letter 'r' told General Frey that his men had mounted the wall of the Imperial Palace during the night, over the Peitang, and had spoken with the missionaries, but had not descended, wanting to leave the liberation of their Mission to the French troops.

Some French soldiers blew up the large gate with a charge but then, from a barricade placed on the way to the Imperial Palace, came a discharge of rifles. The General ordered the artillery to be placed in position to blast away the barricade, which was about one hundred meters from us but the short Japanese captain asked permission to storm it with his soldiers, without waiting for the French artillery and, singing a song which they told me was their cry of *banzai*, he ran towards the barricade with about one hundred of his small soldiers, crooked like him, who advanced under Chinese fire to the admiration of the Europeans. About twenty of those Japanese remained on the ground but the rest - in a few minutes - reached the target: we heard a scream, and there was no trace of those Chinese. At the Petang the survivors welcomed their liberators with joy. Olivieri was still sick because of head wounds and six of our marines were dead.

Here I have reported some anecdotes which impressed me, this may explain why the first singular person is recurring too often while, during the Siege, I had no occasion to do more than any of the other Ministers.

The man who distinguished himself in an admirable way was Livio Caetani, and the foreigners never ceased to mention him in a flattering way: he honored our Country and the diplomatic corps.

I thought that, with the arrival of our troops, our existence in Beijing would become once more agreeable but I was wrong.

We were piled up one over the other but during the Siege we were unaware of that. As soon as we were free, that way of living became unbearable. I was forced to send away my wife, her nerves being too shaken and because I came to realize that there was no way to let a lady and a child stay in that city full of decomposing bodies, infested by repulsive swarms of flies and without a lodging, since our Legation had been destroyed.

Sir Claude sent his sister-in-law with the girls to Tianjin on guarded boats and I took that same chance with my wife, who travelled with Livio Caetani, who was sick. Kindly our Royal Navy put at their disposal the warship Calabria and they reached Japan in not very good health conditions but bit by bit they recovered, thanks to the kind cure of Mr. Cobianchi, commercial attaché at our Embassy and the doctor of the Calabria, who was appointed by the captain to take care of them. During the month of December my wife and Livio Caetani returned to Italy.[80]

The day after the liberation of the Petang, while all Ministers were meeting to discuss the situation, my valet announced the arrival of the *Commander of the Italian troops.*

I stood up to see who this commander might be, not knowing anything about it and I found facing me a tall, brown haired, very thin, young man with a long beard and abundant hair. He was wearing a khaki uniform and high boots, like those of Russian officers, holding in his hands a cowboy hat. His appearance was not reassuring, and it seemed I was facing an adventurer who had joined the International troops, certainly he could not be a navy officer! I enquired who he was and what he wanted, possibly not in a cordial tone. He began to say that having learned that I was a smoker of

---

80. Possibly during their return something romantic happened. Years later Camilla Salvago Raggi told her daughter-in-law that, after she had become pregnant with their son, Paris, she had not had any further physical contact with her husband.

Italian Warship Elba

cigarettes he had thought to give me a box. Realizing that I had not understood who he was he repeated his name, his position and added that he had come from Tianjin together with the German and Austrian contingent. That's was how I met Sirianni.[81] The offer of cigarettes soon lead to a certain liking and our work together for the 14 following months left me with a deep impression of respect and fondness for such a capable young officer who, at the head of thirty marines within the Seymour expedition corps, had proved able to win himself and his soldiers the commendations of the British Admiral.

During the Siege of Tianjin he had gained the admiration of all; and in spite of the fact that the Captain of the warship Elba had discouraged an advance towards Beijing with few men tired after two months of fighting, he had wanted to mix

81. Giuseppe Sirianni 1874-1955). During the war between Italy and Turkey in 1912 he commanded the torpedo boat *Perseo* in the Dardanelles. In WWI he was in command of several warships and between June-October 1918 he participated with his marines in front line operations. From 1929 until 1933 he was Italy's Minister of the Navy.

with the foreign troops in order to let Italy be represented at the taking of Beijing, demonstrating a serene courage, gaining the respect of his men which would be shown again in the coming years, during his expedition to the Dardanelles and the command of the San Marco regiment on the Isonzo River during WWI.

My first concern, as soon as my family had left, was to abandon the British Legation where I felt out of place, so notwithstanding the courteous insistences of MacDonald, I moved with Sirianni and the marines under his command, after the departure of Paolini to Japan, to a corralled place where there was a sort of canopy covered with imperial yellow tiles and closed on three sides. I learned later that it was a sort of oratory where once a year the Emperor goes to pray, facing the tablets of his ancestors which are buried in Manchuria. It was, if I understood well, a sort of fake grave where the Emperor discharged his filial duties. It was the only building still standing in the neighborhood of the Legations quarter and I selected it because it was located on a piece of land of about one hectare, with a low wall around and in a place which looked to me to be suitable for the future Italian Legation. The marines divided my part of the canopy using wooden frames covered by Korean paper found in an abandoned shop and in that way, I had three rooms: one meeting room, one on the left for my study and one on the right where Sirianni and I slept under blankets saved from the Siege. Then I got from the MacDonalds a complete bed; Sirianni and I played *la morra* (odd and even with the fingers) to decide who would get the metallic net of the bed, and who the mattress on the floor, and we lived like that until we got two real beds, blankets and covers from Shanghai.

At the beginning we were getting, for both the marines and for us, two rations of food from the British orderly; but the prolongation of that life on credit was embarrassing, until the resourceful Sirianni put an end to it, coming back one evening with a cart loaded with grain, two mules and a herd of bleating sheep. The marines organized a mill, also an oven, and after that we ate bread and boiled sheep-meat.

The diplomatic corps met regularly to regulate the still uncertain situation in Beizhili[82]. The Court had fled to Shanxi. In Beijing were troops from the United States, France, Japan and Germany, which, having repelled the Chinese soldiers had remained temporarily in the city. The Summer Palace, at a few kilometers from the city, had been occupied by the Russian soldiers. All the Legations were receiving instructions from their Government to regulate the occupation of Beijing, control the operation of the railway and regularize the conduct of relations with the Chinese Government. Only one Legation was not receiving instructions at all: that of Italy!

The disinterest of the Ministry for the poor Royal Embassy of Italy was such that the American Minister first and then, one by one, all the Ministers, circulated congratulatory telegrams received from their governments, with greetings for their representatives, to the personnel and the other Ministers for having escaped such great danger. I, who had received nothing, faked a telegram from our Minister, Visconti Venosta, so kind toward our colleagues which, once it went around, provoked letters of thanks for the kind expression of thanks from the Italian Government.

All the powers seemed to be in accord when it came to want to start peace negotiations with the Chinese Government, but first we needed to assure public order in the city and in the provinces.

---

82. Northern Zhili (Bei Zhili). The name Zhili means *directly ruled* and indicates regions directly governed by the imperial government of China. Zhili province was first set during the Ming Dynasty when the capital of China was located at Nanjing known as Southern Zhili (Nan Zhili) along the Yangtze River. In 1403, the Yongle Emperor moved the capital to Beiping, which was subsequently renamed Beijing (literally, "Northern capital"). The region known as Northern Zhili (Bei Zhili) was composed of parts of the modern provinces of Hebei, Henan, Shandong, and the administrative districts of Beijing and Tianjin.

To regulate all the pending matters a meeting with all the Ministers and the Military commanders was convened. I went together with Sirianni, the only Italian officer in charge of our 32 marines.

Ambassador of France Pichon, with the rifle

During that meeting, it was decided to divide the Tartar City into several areas, over which each one of the military corps would take charge. Seeing them tracing the areas on a map I asked which one would be reserved for 'the Italian troops'. My question surprised my colleagues who did not know that there were Italian troops in China. Even if I was not aware of their presence I had heard from a British officer that he read in a Singaporean newspaper that Italian troops directed to China were on the way and since that news may have been true I thought it proper to reserve for them a place not inferior to the others.

My colleagues brought to my attention the fact that, when an area was reserved for the Italian contingent, we should guarantee law and order in that area. Despite the pulling of my jacket made by Sirianni, I answered that the soldiers already in the Bei Zhili and those I was waiting for would ensure the security in the assigned quarter.

As I expected, they gave us an area they did not want to have: The North-West corner of the Tartar City, inhabited by poor people and up to then not occupied by foreign troops. Sirianni, who at the beginning had tried to point out to me the difficulty of taking charge of that area with only 32 marines, then understood why I had spoken like that and he set to work at it.

After breakfast, we went to find horses for our marines and with some of them, transformed into cowboys, we captured a number of those which had been abandoned in Beijing. In two or three hours, we had captured many, among which we selected a dozen of the best and easier to tame. Then we set to produce, using ropes, some bridles, belts and stirrups; with blankets, we prepared saddles. Truly that day I came to admire the cleverness of our sailors.

Sirianni and I went with our horses to explore the quarter assigned to Italy which I did not know, since it did not contain any temple nor monuments but only dwellings of poor families and had never been a place for merry tourism.

A bit ashamed of our looks and our mounts I chose the northern way along the wall of the Imperial Palace, where we had less chance of meeting Europeans. To be prudent, since I was not sure what kind of a welcome we would receive in that quarter, not knowing if the invading troops had already entered it, I decided to stay on the main roads where the relative speed of our horses would have given us an advantage over the mob, leaving us some chance to escape, since we were only two men with two revolvers.

But we had no problem with the population since all the inhabitants of the future Italian quarter must have remained locked inside their poor dwellings, with only a few of them outside who were indeed not dangerous: they were kneeling at the passage of the *Italian army* and their behavior made us glad, a gladness we did not possess at the onset of our exploration.

On reaching the Sicemen (the gate of the city which I had selected as the first place to occupy) we noticed a machine gun on one of the sloops giving access to the upper part of the door which, once appropriated, could deter people with wrong ideas. We returned home, and then Sirianni placed some of our marines at that gate when it was already dark, so that others could not see how few the Italians were guarding it.

When he returned late in the night he told me that all was quiet in our territory; I breathed a sigh of relief when, in the morning, I went there alone (because Sirianni was not feeling well, after having spent several hours on a horse, which was not the usual mode of travel for a navy officer) to see how our marines had spent the night. I found them in good spirits.

The same day we received the contingent commanded by Lieutenant Sambuy[83]and that marked the end of my taking care of our military occupation of Beijing.

---

83. Luigi Balbo di Bertone Sambuy (1873-1945).

Vincenzo Garioni

X

The occupation of the city happened quickly. As I have mentioned, a few hours after the arrival of General Gaselee at the British Legation, only a few Chinese units were spotted running away around the Legations. There was no attempt to organize a resistance in some parts of the city, and therefore we could have easily proceeded to a calm and orderly occupation, avoiding violence and the sacking carried out by all foreign soldiers. But two circumstances had prevented it: the arrival, almost at the same time, of troops belonging to different countries; then, the poor and desperate people around the city, that afternoon of August 15 and during the following days.

The commanders of the different units had on the 14th a single purpose: to be the first to enter Beijing. The preoccupation of each of them had been solely to occupy the largest portion of the city: therefore, a great freedom of action was left to the lesser officers in charge of each of the small units and there was a true race, within Beijing, a race which did not favor discipline.

After the race to occupy the largest area of the city came the race to occupy the best quarters, and for several units it was a cause of anger to find Japanese sentinels to be the first to claim buildings, where banks and exchange offices, or pawn houses, were located. The Japanese, being able to read Chinese characters, were also able to choose first and better than all the others.

This race to the banks was the result of the wish of many of the officers to ensure that the enemy's funds came under their administration…, but I cannot exclude the fact that in many of them, since the beginning or perhaps later, due to emulation, a more egoistic and less patriotic motive was at work.

We could see soldiers carrying sacks full of silverware. Were they going to their command posts? I don't know and I don't believe so.

The same happened with the pawn shops and the warehouses. But, as I was saying, part of the reason for the sack was due to the general condition of the city in those days.

At sunrise on the 15 of August, the Court was fleeing North. If the various expedition corps, instead of having the exclusive preoccupation of entering the city all together, would have all moved under a single flag, they would have attacked a single or more points of the wall and would have sent some cavalry to get around the city. In that case they would have captured the fleeing Empress, even if I can't be sure that, from a political point of view, this would have been better.

Once the Court had departed, all the local authorities followed; the military commanders and also the few remaining soldiers took off their jackets with the regiment insignia (their only uniform) and morphed into common citizens, whereupon the poorest people joined in sacking everything. Our troops, spreading into the city, made them flee but found that the sack had already begun. I remember having seen, on the evening of the 15, the road that led from the most southern gate to the great Hatamen Alley[84] full of rolls of silk, of embroidered dresses and very beautiful furs taken from the shops, certainly before the arrival of the Europeans, and pulled on the road by Chinese looters who then fled, on seeing our soldiers.

All such goods, left under the rain, would have been spoiled. Some military commanders decided to collect them with the aim of having them auctioned later. The move seemed logical and justified but it conveyed the message that looting was all right.

---

84. Chongwenmen Dajie

If these military people then took pleasure in their task and had it carried on as a private business, I would not have been surprised, just as all those who had seen what humanity can do in time of war would not have been surprised either. In the absence of a military police force able to understand the basic difference between what belongs to us, and what belongs to others, and when one has a loaded rifle in his hands with the license to kill his own neighbor, then, anything can happen.

Certainly, discipline can hold people back but there is no doubt that the difference in character among different nationalities can make the difference even if... I can't give my advice to people with women, children or goods, to stay close to troops at war, no matter their nationality.

As the official and unofficial sack were proceeding, there was also some violence. The foreign soldiers, at the beginning, were unable to distinguish between military and civilians; after all, as I have said, the military were quick to abandon their pins and it was not easy thus to shoot only at the military. The instruction to shoot civilian looters was also given, but it was easy to mistake peaceful citizens, returning to their homes, for robbers. By mistake, certainly not intentionally, a group of Japanese soldiers shot at me while I was looking for a spot to be used as living quarters between the Hatamen and the Legation quarter. When you start to shoot, it is not easy to stop and, I repeat, in war the value of human life is greatly diminished since it is so easy to clip it.

I cannot exclude, therefore, the possibility that some of the dead bodies which we frequently found in the streets of Beijing during these first days, instead of being Boxers or Chinese soldiers, may have been peaceful citizens. But there were no true massacres.

Only in one quarter were women and children murdered: The Western quarter of the Hatamen Road, between Yongdinmen and the Observatory, which had been taken at the beginning by the Russians. A secretary of the Yamen who had always been on friendly terms with us came during the first days with tears in his eyes and told us facts which were sorrowful, which had happened in the quarter where he was living. I went there and I saw some children with their heads broken and some women naked and killed, probably after having been raped. It is the only occasion of grave violence which I came to know.

Let me conclude that it would also have been desirable to deny what I have admitted here but it is certain that reports reaching Europe contained a lot of exaggeration. They were exaggerated because men love exaggeration, because many wanted to cast a dark shadow on the Army, and there were exaggerations because people who live peacefully in their homes in comfort and tranquility, their safe civilian lives, cannot realize the mentality of soldiers who suffer hardship, who run the danger of being killed and then reach a city where men, women and children of their own race have been massacred, starved to death and made to suffer, by order of a Government made by barbarous and cruel men.

Years later, [I got a confirmation of my pessimism] discussing this with women who had been locked up with us during the Siege, I asked them to tell me what the soldiers should have done if they would have been in command. Good and peaceful ladies, whose orders would have then been issued *at the time of the liberation* when their memories of the fear, of the danger of losing their lives, and the torture of women of their race were still fresh in their memories.

I am, on the other hand, more than anybody else, able to judge dispassionately the behavior of the liberating troops during the first days of the occupation, because there were no Italians soldiers around. Our few marines who emerged alive from the Siege, or those participating in the Seymour's expedition, from the fight in Tianjin and the march on Beijing, had only three desires: to rest, have their wounds tended, and regain their strength. They had to take care of their daily chores: providing three sentry services and three guard services.

Certainly, private property and that of the Court suffered greatly. As I said the Summer Palace was first occupied by Russians. Then, following the policy which the Saint Petersburg government wanted them to follow, Russian troops were withdrawn, and we learned that the Summer Palace was evacuated. The Minister of Great Britain decided to send his troops there and he said to me that, if I wanted to send some of our marines to participate to the occupation I was free to do it: I accepted immediately, because I thought that could be useful to enhance our image in the Far East. For the same reason, I then made sure that Italian units were participating in all expeditions made in Bei Zhili and with great effort I managed to have an Italian officer - Germans were opposed to it - inside the provisional Government of the city of Tianjin. Therefore, I sent a unit of marines under the command of Lieutenant Colli di Felizzano to the Summer Palace, together with British soldiers.

Our troops were installed in the apartments where several pieces of furniture remained, but in some of the halls they found three or four hundred wooden crates, sealed, on which were written some addresses in Russian; the crates were numbered but the numbers were starting from 383, which meant that 382 had already been taken away. When we handed over the Summer Palace, unfortunately, it was not as we had found it because we had made the mistake (perhaps we could not do otherwise) to allow Europeans inside, civilians and military, and they did not always behave irreproachably. But all the crates found were returned intact, and others filled with small objects were found by our men in other halls of the palace. The surprised Chinese authorities could not understand why we were returning them. I don't know what was inside the crates, but I believe there were small pieces of furniture, porcelain, and knick-knacks.

The American Minister: Mr Edwin Conger

The German Minister: Baron von Ketteler

Paris Salvago Raggi in Peking

XI

The Forbidden City was the real Imperial Palace, where French and British had not set foot in 1860, had also not been taken by the troops entering Beijing in 1900.

The Palace was guarded by Court officials. Doors were not opening, and communications were carried out with baskets lowered down from the walls; that was also the system used to feed those inside.

What should we have done? Respect the Palace, not enter it until the signing of a peace treaty? Or occupy it?

To give you an idea of the mentality of those times, I will add that there was also the proposal - not even discussed, anyway – to take all artistic pieces it contained and then blow it up or burn it down, as a punishment for the Infringement of the human rights of the Europeans made by the Empress. The more peaceful wanted to respect it and not even step inside it.

Some feared that the Chinese would have repeated what they had done after the 1860's occupation, suggesting that the *Western barbarians, terrorized while facing the image of the Son of Heaven, did not dare to step inside.*

I confess that I believed we should make a sort of symbolic act of possession of the Palace, and I also confess today that I was wrong and that it was a big mistake.

The Dynasty *lost face,* and perhaps also our entrance in the Imperial palace had contributed in part to the downfall of the Manchu Dynasty, a deplorable thing, since it has been replaced by a Republic.

Perhaps we should have completed the downfall of the Dynasty. Then the coming of the Republic could have been staved off. But it is easy to evaluate past events with the wisdom of hindsight, we should have had a new dynasty ready and, lastly (a circumstance graver than the others) there were too many powers deciding. A lot of talks went on at that time about a *European concert,* but I believe that never there was a concert so much out of tune. In 1919, there was enough common sense not to use the word *concert* to indicate the Ministers meeting at Versailles. We decided then to make an act of taking possession of the Imperial Palace, while respecting it above all to safeguard the collections which it contained, which had a great importance for Chinese Arts in general.

Such a wise proposition was carried out following the following program: we, the Ministers, should present ourselves at the main gate on the South, together with some troops. Such force should be important, following the number of military forces present in the capital at that time.

We would then order those inside to open the doors, and we would then enter, followed by the military and we would reach, *without stopping,* the Northern Gate. The troops would come up parading in front of us and we would then go out asking those responsible to close the Gate at our back so that no *European would have entered again into the Imperial Palace.*

The program was good enough and contained the concept of taking possession, as well as the defense of the integrity of the Palace and of the art collections it contained. But God who had created man in His image wanted to give him a partner, and He created the woman!

At the Winter Palace I had several occasions to convince myself of such truth. All had gone well, with great dignity. Those eunuchs who showed us the way to follow should have felt that we were the representatives of civilized and honored countries. But on the North side we found the ladies waiting for us, who had wanted to see the troops marching and put their noses in the last courtyard of the Palace. I don't know who had opened the Northern Gate for them.

The troops marched and we needed to get out behind

them, but the descendants of the first partner created by the manipulation of a rib taken from our first father, the descendants of greedy Eve, were there and their men were weak. They wanted to see, to have a look at the Imperial Palace, which no European had seen after Fr. Matteo Ricci and his Jesuits. The Ministers did not get out but went back with their families, with some foreigners joining, some officers, some correspondents of newspapers, and they visited every corner of the Palace.

A few souvenirs disappeared, and along with them, also our dignity, the majesty of the ceremony, but perhaps I am too critical, because my family had left already and at the Italian Legation there were no women. The door of the violation of the program had been left ajar: it had had to open several times since that day.

Marshal Waldersee obtained permission to stroll into the Palace. Then was the turn of other minor officers and finally there was a day of the week during which the Palace was open to all *distinguished* people.

Objects of modest dimensions came out hidden in the pockets of the visitors and larger pieces were smuggled out by the guardians, who had been bribed. In the sitting room of an American lady in Beijing (Ms. Squiers)[85] I had admired a block of wonderful jade finely engraved, at least eighty or ninety centimeters tall, and of forty or fifty wide. A single block! I heard that, when the Empress wanted to return in the Palace, the Chinese Ministers offered hundreds of thousands of francs to her, trying to have it back. It was an historic relic which had been for centuries in the private apartment of the Emperor. Unfortunately, the generous offers made by the Chinese further convinced the greedy American lady to have made a good deal. She had confided to me that she had obtained it with the gift of a case of whisky made

---

85. Harriet Bard Squiers, wife of Herbert Godsmith Squiers (1859-1911), the Secretary at the American Legation. They had 3 children at the Siege.

to soldiers of her country who had been guarding the Gate and had struck up a friendship with some servants in the Palace. All this is shameful, I know, but how many times I have heard expressions of regret, compassion and reproach because I have no Chinese objects in my home[86]! But I cannot congratulate myself for this. I was alone, I had a lot of work to do, I was unable to 'collect' and I had no troops riding for me. Then, when it was possible to buy with little money precious objects, I refused to do it because I had to set an example when dressing down my fellow citizens who were perhaps too passionate about the *art of collecting*. It is not for me to boast about anything. I did not want to, but I also had less chances than others, and before blaming others we need to be sure that, in the same conditions we would have behaved better than those we criticize. It seems, even if I had been in their circumstances, I believe that I would have behaved better, but can I state that with a clear conscience?

---

86. In 2016 I visited Giuseppe Salvago Raggi's villa at Campale. It was a bit like being in a museum of Chinese art. Camilla, his granddaughter, had asked Pippo about their provenance and he told her that they were all bought and paid, not in Beijing. This has to be true because the majority of those artworks are *Chine de commande* which were not available in Beijing.

XII

I have reviewed the previous pages and it comes naturally to me to think that if, from the first day of the Siege moving forward, we Ministers had been involved in diplomacy or rather in all possible professions except diplomacy. In fact, I was promoted Secretary of the Legation of first class with the credentials of Minister upgraded to that of extraordinary envoy and plenipotentiary with the responsibility of a full Minister!

While in Cairo, I had discharged my duty to the satisfaction of the Ministry, but I had not been promoted! It is not my intention to complain here of not having been promoted at that time, a promotion which was not due to me, since I had just discharged my duty with honor but nothing more than that.

I find it funny to think that, in Beijing, when I did my job as a diplomat, they were not happy with me to the point that - I learned later - they were ready to recall me. But as soon as I began to do a lot of things which had nothing to do with diplomacy, then I was promoted.

I received also the title of Commander of the order of the St. Maurizio and Lazzaro, quite an honor for a second-class diplomat as well also for a first secretary, which gave me a certain amount of pride.

But the thing which compensated me for all the trouble I had suffered was a telegram from King Vittorio Emanuele III. If I had to be put through the Siege again (without my family) I would have gladly accepted, to feel a bit less guilty for not really having deserved that telegram.

Some believe that the Empress Dowager came to realize her mistake of having made an alliance with the Boxers well before the foreign troops entered Beijing. This opinion was justified by the publication, at the beginning of August, when the foreigners were already in charge of Tianjin and strong enough to march on the capital, of an imperial edict stating that Li Hongzhang had been nominated minister plenipotentiary.

I am not convinced of that. The Empress had made an alliance with the Boxers hoping they would massacre all of the Europeans in Beijing. Then, she would have declared to the Powers that she had done the impossible to save us but her troops had been overwhelmed by that unexpected popular insurgency. Finally, she would have concluded that being un able to guarantee the safety of the Foreign Ministers, if they insisted on staying in China, it would be necessary for them to move to Shanghai. A solution which would have contributed, according to the Chinese mentality, to the great success of her reign.

At the beginning of August, the Empress knew that we were at the end of our provisions and she had issued an order to double the violence of the attacks. The mines under the British Legation were about to be lit and she had confidence that the massacre of the Legations was close at hand, thus ending the Siege.

Once this had happened no surviving person could have disputed her version of the events about the killing of the diplomats, and that would have been the right time to discuss peace terms, with the subsequent removal of the Legations under the protection of cannons of the warships. Anyway, the fact was that old Li Hongzhang had already been nominated plenipotentiary for peace when troops entered Beijing and he asked us for permission to return to the capital. An imperial decree dated from Shanxi nominated Prince Qing as the head of the Chinese mission for discussing peace. The poor prince, already accused of being a xenophile had trembled all his time during the Siege, afraid to pay for all. He wanted to see all the Ministers, but he had some problem to come and see me, because my residence was in an ancient Oratory of his family. I went to stay there ignoring that detail but I had no other place to go and, therefore, I answered that I did not choose that residence but I had to take advantage of the only construction in that area which had been left standing by the Chinese troops. If he did not want to come, no problem, he could discuss with the others and not with me. But he came and he agreed with me about the ferocity of his Government, he denied having ever signed certain petitions which we had received during the Siege, to lure us in to a trap and he agreed with me that they had been just snares. Then he left, begging me to stop all hostilities.

That day the diplomatic corps was meeting to discuss the conditions to apply to China and at the same time the unofficial contacts with Li Hongzhang were proceeding. It was at that time that he came to ask me not to insist on the liberation of certain missionaries, a condition I had imposed to stop the march of a certain battalion of Italian troops towards a place which he wanted us to spare.

He insisted, but I had committed myself to an alternative: either they would take the actions I had demanded, or the battalion would carry on. Li Hongzhang, furious, began to say that certainly these were not the instructions I had received from my King, that he knew him, and he was a courteous person, a compassionate man, an educated person. He continued by giving me a list of all the qualities of the Italian King, implicitly alluding to the fact that I was the contrary of him, but I could not take offence, because he was praising my Sovereign. That amused the other Chinese who had followed Li, and their smiles were an eloquent proof of it, while I was lost for an answer. At the end, I told him that he had met my King only once, while I met him several times, therefore it was of no use for him to give me such a list of his qualities, an incomplete list anyway, because he was aware of only half of his Kingly merits and I could reveal to him several more. Then, I prayed that he would stop and go away, because I was very busy. The old rogue wanted to stop our troops but, in the end, he had to do what I was asking him to do. The missionaries who had survived the massacres in Shanxi were thus set free. In the future, finding myself in a similar situation, I told him that it was useless to give me a list of the qualities of my King since it would not stop me from doing what I wanted.

At the end of September Prince Qing and Li gave us a decree they had submitted to the Emperor which indicated that China was accepting the blame of the princes belonging to the imperial family who had allied with the Boxers: they also wanted to punish them and open a discussion.

The ideas of the various Ministers were different: some wanted the head of the Empress, and some did not want to see any capital punishment for those guilty of the massacres. M. de Giers one day declared that his Government was against the death penalty...because of political reasons.

Pichon, who despite the alliance, was always in disagreement with M. de Giers about Chinese matters, confessed that he was, generally speaking, against the death penalty and he would like it to disappear from the French penal code for all crimes, with the exception of political crimes: "Car je suis dans les bonnes traditions de notre grande révolution."

In conclusion, time was passing and the European concert... was out of tune. Finally, after several months (if I am not mistaken it was Christmas Eve) we did manage to put together an answer signed by all of us. I remember that at the end we could not agree on the top of our letter and I proposed a note, which I wrote on the corner of the table with a pencil, which was accepted: "Pendant les mois de mai, juin, juillet et aôut de cette année des crimes sans précedents dans l'histoire, des crimes contre le droit des gens, contre les lois de l'humanité et contre la civilisation ont été commis etc."

The period was accepted and Pichon whispered quietly:

"Je ne sais pas si Voltaire l'aurait signé, moi comme il parait que l'on l'accept je vous en félicite."

With that document, which did not appear to have been written while Angels in the sky were singing "peace to the world", because we were putting some severe conditions under which peace could be accepted, the Chinese, within two or three days, published an imperial decree wholly accepting all the conditions..., but the treaty was signed only nine months later. The delay was not due to ill intentions of the Chinese but mainly because of the misunderstandings among the eleven Governments involved.

During those negotiations, I had briefly entertained the hope of being able to revive our negotiations, since the discussions on Sanmen Bay had never been officially closed.

I went on board to speak about it with Admiral Candiani.[87] It was an invitation to a wedding for him!

Admiral Camillo Candiani, commander of the Italian contingent in China

---

87. Camillo Candiani D'Olivola (1841-1919). As a junior officer, he had served on the ship *Magenta* commanded by Capt. Arminjon, which departed from Naples on 8 November 1865 for a tour around the world. During their stop in China they signed the first treaty between Italy and China. He retired from active duty in 1910.

We did agree that he would temporarily occupy Nimrod with the pretext to move his sick sailors there and protect them from the winter of Bei Zhili, very harsh for us, Southern people. That pretext was funny because the conditions of all our sailors were excellent: the percentage of sick people was lower than for the other troops, but we did not publish the data and the news of our occupation. Incidentally I informed my colleagues as a detail with no importance. No one objected to that. We had to inform the Ministry as a formality, for 'sanitary' reasons. Then, further on, I could return to it about the possibility to remain in Nimrod forever.

I had no time to move to phase two because the Minister of Foreign Affairs, Prinetti[88] (who perhaps understood my intentions) informed me that there was an agreement with all Governments not to take advantage of China's poor predicament for unlimited occupations etc.

That irritated me, but I had to realize that it was a correct decision and that agreement was right and proper to let the *European concert* carry on with the music, even if not properly tuned.

I had more luck with the settlement in Tianjin. As is well known, Italy had no settlements in China. The Russians in those days had occupied an area between the railway and the river to transform it into a settlement. I thought that we could occupy the neighboring zone and, thinking it difficult to explain to the Ministry the difference between the occupation of a territory and an area already open to commerce, on the other hand thinking that we had to move quickly, I decided to carry on with the occupation 'on behalf of the Legation' and then inform the Ministry, explaining the importance to carry on with the definitive occupation. If

---

88. Giulio Nicolò Prinetti Castelletti (1851-1908). A conservative politician and industrialist. With his brother-in-law, Augusto Stucchi, he founded a company producing bicycles and cars: it was there that Augusto Bugatti made his first steps as a mechanic. In 1901, he became Minister of Foreign Affairs in the Zanardelli - Giolitti Government.

the Ministry would have replied disagreeing with it, it would have then been easy to explain that I wanted that land as a deposit for material and as a place for our soldiers to camp.

Mario Valli[89] was put in charge of the occupation for the Legation of Italy. All was going well until Giers came to protest. Apparently, his consul was upset, having been reproached because he had taken only a small portion of the future Russian settlement and wanted more, but now was limited in his options because of our move. I could not back off and we ended up exchanging some not very cordial propositions. Luckily Giers did not know that at that time it had been solely my decision and the Ministry in Rome would have been very surprised if the Russian Government would have lodged a formal protest. They did not do it, and all died there, with a small discussion between us.

Fortunately for us, Giulio Prinetti was then the Minister of Foreign Affairs: he knew what a settlement was, and he was not afraid of it. He sent a telegram allowing the occupation but reserving the right to regularize the legal situation in the future with the Chinese Government.

In the meantime, the agreement for a peace treaty was proceeding slowly because of the differences between the allies, and the Chinese were taking advantage of it to avoid the conditions we had put forward.

Our discussions for the punishments were very curious. We had several misunderstandings between us, because we

---

89. Mario Valli (1867-1918) was from an illustrious family of Narni. His brothers were all successful: Giannetto Valli became Mayor of Rome in 1922; Giulio Valli (1875-1949), was an Admiral of the Navy, director of the aeronautic academy of Italy and a Senator; Luigi Valli (1878-1931) was a writer and a poet.
Their father was Candido Valli (1835-1912), the owner of a large company building railways and palaces.
The Valli beautiful villa is still visible in Narni, it is called Villa Montiello. Mario Valli published a detailed book on the Italian participation in the Boxer's war: *Gli Avvenimenti in Cina nel 1900 e l'azione della Regia Marina Italiana,* Hoepli, Milan, 1905 and also *Attraverso la Mongolia - note di viaggio,* Nuova Antologia, Rome 1902, about his return trip from Beijing to Italy, together with Giuseppe Salvago Raggi.

had problems identifying the responsibilities of the guilty. Most of them, or better say those with whom we had reached a sort of consensus, were considered the main culprits. Prince Tuan, official head of the Boxers and he was, perhaps, the man responsible for all the support given to the Boxers and possibly the one who had ordered the murder of all the Ministers, a plan which had worked fine only for the German Representative. Duke Lan, head of the police and author of the decree which we found posted on the roads, promising 50 taels to those who would carry to him a European man, 40 for a woman, and 30 each for the children. Kang-Yi[90], who let the Boxers enter the city. Yuxian, ex-Governor of Shanxi: a sort of ogre, who had murdered with his own hands some missionaries who were his prisoners and five or six more Europeans.

But the difficulty of obtaining the death penalty for all of them was great: Prince Tuan was a close relative of the Emperor and father of the heir to the throne. One of the main culprits was certainly Dong Fuxiang,[91] a General, therefore the Court would have not hesitated to concede his head, since in China the military did not enjoy much prestige. But he was in command of 10,000 soldiers who were loyal to him. It was easy to condemn him but difficult to catch him.

Then there were difficulties on agreeing on the names of the people who had been less prominent. Some thought that they knew of horrible deeds carried out by so and so and were asking for the death penalty, others thought that they knew somebody else who had done worst. There were negotiations on the death penalty, and to grant the death penalty to a certain Chinese instead of another become a sort

---

90. Grand Secretary Kang-Yi was one of the most radical supporters of the Boxers, together with Prince Tuang.

91. Dong Fuxiang (1839–1908) was a Chinese General. He was born in the western Chinese province of Gansu and commanded an army of Hui soldiers, which included General Ma Anliang and Ma Fuxiang.

of personal favor. We finally reached some sort of agreement when the good Conger, following information received from missionaries, demanded the head of Ka-sien[92], and Conger came to me telling that he was missing only my consensus to sign the final agreement. On his account, he could only tell me that, according to American missionaries, he was one of the main culprits. Truly, to agree on beheading a man his word was not enough, and although he was a Chinese who had been implicated in all the affairs, and even with the mentality common in those days, I hesitated. But we had to reach an agreement and so I agreed to the death of the unknown Ka-sien.

To tell the truth, I had thought that between agreeing with him on being put in the list and have his head cut off there was still time to go, and I committed myself to do some investigation into the case. During the next days we did it, using sources different from those used by Conger. From the results, it was apparent that Ka-sien was really one of the main culprits and he had caused the death of four Chinese Ministers who had tried to warn the Government about the dangers of associating with the Boxers. I did not withdraw my consent for his execution.

During the months of February and March, the eleven Ministers of our civilized countries engaged in discussions with the Chinese plenipotentiaries about the way to punish the guilty people. On the one side the Chinese admitted their

---

92. Ka-sien(?) perhaps Yü Hsien. Protestant and Catholic missionaries and their Chinese parishioners were massacred, some by Boxers and others by government troops and authorities. Yü Hsien, governor since the month of March, implemented a brutal anti-foreign and anti-Christian policy. On 9 July he had executed forty-four foreigners from missionary families whom he had invited to the provincial capital Taiyuan promising to protect them. More foreigners and as many as 2.000 Chinese Christians had been put to death in the province. Journalist and historical writer Nat Brandt have called the massacre of Christians in Shanxi "the greatest single tragedy in the history of Christian evangelicalism." Even if Roger Thompson points out that the widely circulated accounts were by people who could not have been at the events.

faults but argued that the penalty should not be tied to the gravity of the crime but mostly to the situation of the culprit.

On the other side, the Western Ministers were uncomfortable with the decision to either opt for 'condemn to suicide' or 'suspended death sentence', punishments which they were not formally asking but ended up bearing responsibility for them, because we did not oppose them and we finally approved them, at least by remaining silent.

Finally, after a long struggle to avoid them, the Court accepted our demands with light changes and an imperial decree condemned Prince Zhang to suicide.[93]

Tuan and Lan were degraded and sent to Mongolia in exile, five or six more were condemned to death or received suspended death sentences.

I bear my part of responsibility, not greater and not lesser than my colleagues for such capital punishments. But, on the other hand, I contributed more than my colleagues - we had to work hard to get it - to concede posthumous honors to the four poor ministers of the Zongli Yamen who had been beheaded for having tried to save us and stop the Chinese Government from moving on the dangerous path it had taken. I consider that it would give a good impression in China the fact that the Western representatives, who were asking with a certain degree of severity the life of some culprits, were also interested in the rehabilitation of others, conferring posthumous honors to those who had tried to serve their Country.

We had then to regulate other questions: forbidding the import of weapons; work for the navigability of the river in Tianjin and others which I don't remember; then the war

---

93. Prince Zhang (1853-1901) hanged himself on 21 February 1901 in Shanxi. Ying Nien and Chao Shu-chiao, Yü Hsien and Hsu Cheng-yu were decapitated. Kang Yi had died and Li Ping-hêng received a posthumous degradation. Dong Fuxiang, one the main culprits, was only degraded. One hundred and nineteen minor officers were sentenced to death. Most of them were freed and could have fled but with great stoicism accepted the Imperial Decree, without any complaint.

indemnities. For Italy, it was set at about three times what we had spent.[94]

I was happy to have been involved in events which had seen the prestige of Italy soar in the Far East, after the Sanmen Bay fiasco and for which not a penny had been wasted.

With the grace of God, the peace treaty was signed (on the 10th, if I remember well).

On this subject I remember a curious anecdote. During the 14 months of negotiation I was informing the Ministry of the progress we were making, and when we all agreed on a clause I telegraphed it to Rome.

When at the end, we had reached a final agreement and we drew up the final document, containing all the single clauses, I asked Rome for permission to sign it, transcribing only the first part. For the remaining clauses, I quoted all the references numbers of the previous telegrams. Clearly, to have the final treaty they just had to line up all my previous telegrams, which I was not retransmitting to save money, since each transmission was 10 gold lire. They just had to take those already sent, following my reference, then copy all in a single document.

It seems that the lazy employee at the Ministry did not want the trouble of reconstructing everything and I don't know how he explained the matter to the Foreign Affairs Minister, who sent me a terrible dressing down in the best Prinetti's style. Prinetti thought it absurd to sign a treaty for which I was not sending the text. I can still see the upset face of Sirianni when he handed me the telegram. I told Sirianni to cypher the complete treaty, then I mounted my horse and went out in the open air to let my anger disperse; I was angry against a colleague who, not wanting to work, was causing me

---

94. Salvago Raggi went through great troubles a few years later, accused by the press and in the Italian Parliament of having inflated the list of his personal losses during the Siege. Salvago Raggi was finally cleared of all charges even if he did not receive a penny as compensation for his personal losses.

an undeserved reproach from the Minister. When I returned, Sirianni and a helmsman were still cyphering it; then I asked them to count the cyphers and multiply by ten lire, getting a very high total. First, I answered the Minister by saying that, to save money, I had not telegraphed the complete text, which could anyway be reconstructed with my old telegrams, without great effort but, but following the Minister's observations, I had cyphered the complete text, which would cost several thousand lire to send and that, without further ado, I would have it sent 24 hours later, in the absence of the receipt of a timely counter-order.

The counter-order arrived before the expiration of the twenty-four hours' period with a telegram marked "Top Urgent", and during the next days a new message which authorized me to sign was received. Months later, when I arrived in Rome, Prinetti remembered that small incident and spoke to me about it, and he exclaimed: "One of those scoundrels who, not wanting to work, was willing to have the Government throw away money!"

Scoundrel was too strong a word, but those who knew Prinetti knew also that he was not stingy on spending insulting words.

My life under that leaking canopy remained unpleasant and not very decent for the good image of the Legation, therefore I asked the Ministry what they wanted me to do about it. If they wanted me to remain I would have tried to find a better place, if they wanted me to depart I would have endured the place until my departure. The Minister answered that as soon as the peace treaty was signed I would be allowed to leave Beijing. On the 9 of September 1901, I was thus able to plan my departure. I had three possibilities: the Indian Ocean route, which I knew already; that via America, which did not attract me greatly; that through Mongolia, which was interesting and had great practical advantages: while on route they would not be able to recall me back to Beijing.

Such danger was not as remote as it seems. Li Hongzhang was very old and sick. He was thought to be the only person on whom the Powers could count in dealing with China, so much so that many thoughts that if he died then the treaty would be cancelled.

A new secretary, already announced during the Spring, had not yet appeared in July. I had asked for news: and the Ministry answered that they were convinced he had already arrived, and they did not know where he might be. Finally, in August, Baron Romano Avezzana[95] arrived in Beijing, coming from Japan, and he was second secretary of the Legation. Before his arrival, I had read in the Italian press the news of his official engagement with a Roman girl and, as soon as I met him, I asked if he was already married, because I was worried that he would ask me for a leave of absence to go back to Italy to marry her, but he answered that he was married and he was waiting for his wife to join him. I finally understood that, while in the United States he had dumped his Roman fiancée and had married instead an American girl, who was following him. He asked for permission to go and visit her in Japan: I agreed, and I asked him to do that as soon as possible. In fact, during the first days of September, he was back in Beijing with his wife.

In the meantime, I received a curious telegram from the Ministry asking me if I thought that Baron Romano Avezzana could handle the Italian Legation alone. I never understood why, having decided that I should leave the Legation, they had sent a Secretary doubting whether he could run the Legation. I replied that before his arrival I had never met him, but during the few days we had spent together in Beijing I got the impression that he was a highly intelligent man. This was true. The telegram from the Ministry and the

---

95. Camillo Romano Avezzana (1867-1949). His wife was Marie Jaqueline Taylor, they had a daughter in Beijing in 1902, Jolanda Romano Avezzana.

Italian warship Vettor Pisani

possible death of Li Hongzhang made me afraid that they would call me back after my departure. I thus decided to avoid that at all costs by putting between me and Beijing a country like Mongolia in winter. I therefore chose that route. The Chinese Government did not like my decision: perhaps because they were afraid that a new incident would have put them in trouble.

I received news that there was no trouble on the road, and I learned from Admiral Candiani that the pleasant officer of the navy with whom I had had several contacts, Mario Valli, would have liked to be my companion. The Admiral was very pleased with that officer and he offered to pay for him out of his own pocket, so that he could accompany me. As a result, I completed my journey in good company. We became close friends and we remained so until his untimely death, which deprived our Navy of a capable officer, and a man of uncommon intelligence and character.

I would not wish to end my memoires of my time in China without recalling the unique figure of Admiral Candiani.

Candiani enjoyed an enormous consideration in the Navy for his qualities, for his energy, and for his very strong initiative. However, he was not known for his obedience to the orders of his superiors. I have collected several anecdotes from the Navy officers I had met. Very characteristic was the story of his participation in the Columbus Day celebrations in Genoa, when he was commanding one of the warships, either the *Italia* or the *Umberto*, the most modern ships of our navy. Captain Candiani, on taking over the command, observed that a golden eagle would have looked nice on the bow, in the shape and dimensions of an eagle he had seen at the La Spezia's Arsenal, inside the military warehouse. He tried to buy it but with no success. When he received the order to go to Genoa, he demanded an additional steam boat to be ready, for the traffic would be intense at the ceremony in Genoa but the Admiralty refused to give it to him.

Candiani had to resign himself to the fact that he must leave without his eagle on the bow and the second steamboat. But resignation was not one of his strong points, and on the day before the departure he asked a worker, who had declared himself capable of attaching the eagle to the bow, how many hours he needed to complete his job, and he had guaranteed six or seven hours. Then he asked him to come on board early in the morning because they had to leave in the afternoon.

He then called a lieutenant, whom he knew to be a capable young man, and he showed him the eagle in the shop of the military union, and told him: "Get it this night and make sure that tomorrow at sunrise you will be on board, but look, if you will be back without the eagle, it will be better for you to get lost."

Then he took an engine driver to the post and let him select the best boat, asking him to get back that evening with two stokers and a sack of coal. From the Arsenal, people who got out with sacks would be a checked to see what they were carrying but entering was no problem. He told him: "At three start the engines and come to port", adding, "I warn you, don't miss it!"

The next morning, Admiral Candiani was departing with his eagle on the bow taken from the Military Union, with a worker on board who was shouting that he wanted to get on dry land and with an additional steamboat which had been taken from the Arsenal. The next day he was entering Genoa, where Candiani's ship looked magnificent with the eagle on her bow. Later the worker, with a good tip in his pocket, took a train back to La Spezia, while an Admiral from the main square of Genoa, happy that the two steam boats provided by Candiani could ferry guests here and there, explained to the Arsenal, and then he told the Arsenal that the seizing of the eagle had been his own decision. This anecdote, which I heard from several marine officers, illustrates well the character of this man. No one could stop him when he wanted something. He had come as division commander, but he snubbed the most senior captain of the *Vettor Pisani,* not hesitating to send him back to Italy, because *he had been too slow* on reaching Tokyo.

When Candiani came to China, he learned that I had not been massacred as it had been reported by the press in Italy, and possibly this news irked him, because he believed that he would be the only man in charge in China. Nevertheless, since he was a very educated person he immediately sent me his greetings, and provided a ship to transport my family to Japan where they remained some days, while the ship's doctor took good care of my wife and my son.

But when Colonel Garioni[96] arrived, with his two battalions, trouble began.

I had thought that, once Beijing was liberated, very little remained to do other than to occupy the Bei Zhili and maintain order, until the signing of the peace treaty, and

---

96. Colonel Vincenzo Garioni (1856-1929).

then depart. In the meantime, I thought for reasons of future prestige it was essential that Italian troops should remain with the others in the capital. French and British soldiers had been in Beijing during the previous years and the Chinese

Mario Valli

knew about them. China was bordering Russia and therefore they were in contact with Russian soldiers. But who knew that Italian soldiers also existed?

With that in mind, I solicited the arrival of our soldiers. Candiani thought otherwise. He wrote to me that he needed the *Bersaglieri* troops to take care of the occupation of ports which the foreign navies had approved. I requested at least a battalion of infantry. At first, Candiani did not answer, using the excuse that he had been to Shanxi. Then, after my insistence, he answered that the infantry battalion was needed in Tianjin. I understood the *Latin,* and I sent a telegram to the Ministry explaining that I thought it important to have the battalions in Beijing, but that the Admiral was refusing. I concluded by asking the Ministry how I should get involved in the deployment of our troops in China. Since the telegraphic line had not been reconnected with Beijing, the telegrams were sent from the ships. I sent the telegram, not ciphered to Candiani, asking him to transmit it to Rome. Candiani read it and he asked me to wait, informing that he was sending an infantry battalion. I agreed, telling him that I was coming to Taku to discuss the matter with him. I went there, and I told him that it was better to reach an agreement between the two of us, because my interests were the same as his interests: to be useful to our Country. I had no antimilitaristic sentiments, even less against the Navy, and I did not want to put my nose into military matters, but I intended to decide about the troops when they had political implications. If he agreed on this point and would not put hurdles in the way, then he could count on me for anything else which was needed for the troops.

We understood each other perfectly, and to everybody's astonishment, we always got along very well. A few days later, Candiani was able to appreciate that a good agreement with me was very useful for him too.

Because of his character, some friction was to be expected

with the other foreign admirals, even considering that the most senior Admiral at Taku was a Russian, with whom Candiani still had some scores to settle from their time in Crete.

When they came to decide upon the occupation of Shan-si Kuan the most senior Admiral, the Russian, having taken command, set the position for the ships. The group of foreign ships should advance along the coast from West to East, keeping thus the coast on the left. The Russian ships were the closest to land, then the others on the extreme right, meaning far away, were the Italians. Candiani observed that in so doing the disembarkation of the Italians would be made after the others, whereas we were the only ones carrying real infantry, and we should have been the first to put them on dry land, but the Russian was adamant. He did not know Candiani well enough.

The ships had to proceed at a speed of ten miles. Candiani, on the Pisani, soon after the start, accelerated to a speed of fifteen, whereupon the Russian sent light signals for him to get back, but Candiani did not see the signals, perhaps taking inspiration from another precedent, even if he had both eyes.

The *Vettor Pisani* reached Shan-xi Kuan before all the others, and the officer put on land his Bersaglieri, who encountered some Chinese soldiers running away and exchanged rifle shots with them. Candiani then chose the most suitable fort, occupied it, left a few officers to facilitate the landing of the other allies, and quietly returned to his ship. I don't know what the Russian Admiral wrote to him, nor what Candiani answered, because when he told me this story Candiani said that his colleague was a bit upset but then he had cooled down.

Later, I received the visit of M. de Giers who strongly complained about the lack of discipline of the Italian Admiral and wanted me *to call him to order*.

I told my colleague that it was not within the tasks of a

diplomat to enter into disciplinary matters of the Navy, and then I added that I cared too much for my career to send a protest to Candiani, who was the honorary *aide de camp* of His Majesty as well as his personal friend and also *aide de camp* of the Duke of Genoa. If he had any complaint about him, it was better to send it through their Ambassador in Rome. In this way Candiani had time to inform his Minister.

The initiatives of Candiani could cause inconveniences, but he had a soft spot. When he heard from me that the reason I wanted the battalions in Beijing was because I wanted all the Chinese to see Italian soldiers, the Admiral understood my meaning, and he started to send to Beijing a complete battalion of marines; then he put on land what he called 'landing companies', a lieutenant or a second lieutenant and a midshipman, with twenty or thirty marines, and with these 'landing units' he colonized the Bei Zhili.

"Make do!" he told them, and those capable young men did make do, guarding half destroyed villages, installing themselves, managing to organize themselves to get supplies, so they kept public order, and it was impossible to go around the Bei Zhili without meeting Italian 'landing units' and thus all thought that we had more troops than those we effectively had. The ships were basically empty, and when one had to sail out of Taku on a mission, a crew was put together taking it from all the other ships, but during the night, so that the other ships would not realize that.

With risks and responsibility, and with sacrifices which he could impose on the other officers and sailors, Candiani did a very good job for our Navy, and during the operations in China he played a greater part than he might have otherwise done, because of the scarcity of men and equipment sent from Italy.

I was always grateful to Candiani, and because of this, I could bear his shortcomings, which were small compared to his great gifts.

Colonel Tommaso Salsa

It was at Nimrod where Candiani gave the best of himself, discharging his duty in a superb manner. As I have already mentioned, I arranged for the temporary occupation of that bay, hoping that we could retain it forever.

The Admiral landed, organized himself on the ground, built barracks for the sailors, explored inland, getting rid of brigands, hunting pirates, having some facing the firing squads, and he organized a marketplace, *forgetting* the existence of the institution of the Customs in China. The population that in a short time saw the commerce flourish, and brigands and pirates disappear, adored him and I am sure that if we had obtained the permission to go ahead from the Ministry to proceed with the final occupation it would have been met by jubilation by the people.

The greatest disappointment for Candiani was that of being sent into retirement with the degree of Rear Admiral for age limits, when he still possessed the energy, the strength and willpower greater than other younger officers. The King appointed him to the Senate, but he went there only a few times, and when I asked the reason, he answered: "What do you want me to do among those good old men? I have always been good at taking action, but there you cannot act, they speak and that had never been my job." By officers and sailors, he was generally adored, but they had to discharge their duty as he ordered; in that case, he was for them like a good father. But with the others he had a heavy hand. Candiani was a leader. Among the officers who came to China there was one who gave me a good impression, Colonel Salsa.[97] Serious, full of energy, intelligent, he gave the impression of knowing well his profession and had all the gifts to do it well.

As soon as I reached Italy I went to stay for a few days in my villa of Campale, because of the health condition of some persons of my family but, as soon as it was possible, I travelled to Rome, where I was received in a flattering way by Minister Prinetti who, even after, remained always well disposed towards me, so much so that his legendary bad temper fits, which I could say I had witnessed, were only directed at other people but never towards me. He was very demanding, and I had a demonstration of it when, during our first talk, after having commended my service in China, he told me to have come to know that I had a fondness for my past posting in Egypt, and that was why he had appointed me as Italy's Diplomatic Agent to Cairo.

Being only first secretary, after having been directly promoted, the posting at Cairo was superior to what I could have hoped. Since I did not want to have a debt of gratitude with the Ministry, and having the impression (perhaps, I was wrong) that the Minister was too patronizing in offering me such a nomination, because of my Genoese character

---

97. Tommaso Salsa (1857-1913) was a very capable officer, who could speak several languages. Many thought that the general command of the Italian Army in China should have been given to him and not to the bearish Vincenzo Garioni.

I answered too coolly to his offer, with a simple: "I agree", words which I tried to pronounce as kindly as I was capable of.

The Minister, thinking that he had been far too generous, (this is true) was expecting from me an explosion of gratitude. Therefore, half upset and half surprised, exclaimed: "I thought you would be glad to be sent to Cairo!"

I tried to explain that I was really very glad about it but I was under the impression that he was not appointing people with the preoccupation of making them happy but, rather thinking what was most useful to the mission, and in that case, I was very glad that the utility for the service coincided with my tastes. I was just unable to thank him too warmly without giving the impression that to please a secretary he had decided on an appointment which was not in the best interest of the service.

The only excuses for my words were my youth, the Siege in Beijing and the 14 months in that *Imperial tomb*.

My attitude too 'Genoese' was appreciated by Prinetti (since he had, like me, a rough character) and who remained, as I said, always well disposed towards me. Even if, at that time, he was upset with me because, with his usual curt manners, told me that I had to leave immediately to reach my post.

After two years in Egypt, with no license, I had left immediately for China; after the first two years in China I had spent 17 days in Italy; I was returning then, after twenty hard months and I was perhaps not wrong to think that it was excessive to be dispatched immediately to my new post.

I just asked: "Now?"

The Minister said that I had to leave by the end of the month. Not wanting to beg for a license, I noted that if the service required me to leave tomorrow, I would dutifully depart, otherwise the internal regulation allowed me a license of six months.

It was at that time that I had the privilege to watch a show of a furious Prinetti. And it was a hell of a show.

His face, rather long, with coarse traits, framed by a short and curly brown beard, became red and from deep red turned violet. His eyes, already large, were growing even larger as if they wanted to jump out of their orbits to attack his victim. His lips, full and chubby, opened showing two rows of very white teeth, big and long, and out of them came with a whistle a: "Six months, you are mad!"

With the greatest calm possible I could muster, I answered: "It am not mad but, if at all, mad are the regulations, which I had not written." Then I confirmed that if it was necessary, I was ready to leave at once.

"The regulations! Where is the book of the regulations?"

I told him I had no copy with me, but I was sure he could find one at the Ministry.

Prinetti hit the bell with a pressure so violent that was like a fist on someone's face.

To his assistant, who had entered the room immediately, he screamed: "Get Malvano here now!"

During the few minutes separating the arrival of Malvano, the Minister was staring at me, rolling his eyes and his bad mood was increasing because I was calmly staring back at him.

Prinetti, tall, strong, violent, was the contrary of Malvano, small, timid, chubby.

The difference between the two became even more noticeable since the furious Prinetti had to scream even louder because Malvano was quite deaf. Malvano stepped in the office and, seeing the storm brewing, would have gladly turned on his heel to leave but not being allowed to do so, he just did a short step forward and uttered: "Oh, dear Salvago…"

But Prinetti cut him down, shouting: "That dear Salvago wants to stay here for six months doing nothing!"

Malvano became suddenly somber, looked at me with a pained expression, as if wanting to say "Oh, I am sorry for what you ask."

I asked him if it was true that our internal regulations allowed me to accumulate a maximum of six months if 'the requirements of our service allowed it?'

The figure of good Malvano, still serious, became a bit less sorry for me and turning to the Minister, this time sorry for him, said that my quote was quite correct.

The fury of Prinetti disappeared with the same speed it had appeared, as soon as the cause was removed.

He calmly asked: "But will you ask for the 6 months leave?"

I confirmed that it all depended on the requirements for my service, that the Minister was the only person who could decide about my leave, and I was waiting for his decision.

We agreed on two months immediately, two more months during the summer and two in the summer of next year. That was the end of the first Prinetti's storm I had watched.

Another happened during the next days, again because of me and I ended up with a new decoration, which I did not expect and left me quite indifferent.

A few months after the Siege of Beijing, the Ministry sent to me a telegram saying that they had come to know that all the Governments were asking their representatives to propose decorations, according to their judgement. In fact, we had discussed this matter in Beijing and we all agreed to avoid exchanges of decorations, as if in an international trade fair, but just propose to decorate those who had really fought to defend the Legations and their actions had effectively saved the Legation of the country which was offering them. I informed the Ministry of our decision to decorate the only two surviving French officers and two Japanese, because at the Peitang they had fought together with our soldiers. The French decorated, besides two of our officers and Caetani,

Four Ambassadors in Peking, from left Italy, Russia, France, Germany.

who had commanded the Italian contingent, two Italian civilians who fought at the French Legation. I did not propose a decoration for Sir Claude Macdonald, even if he had been the commander, because I knew that the British cannot accept decorations coming from foreign countries, but I asked the Ministry to write a letter, thanking him for his hospitality.

A brusque telegram from the Ministry told me that I had

just proposed four or five decorations, while the others, like the French Government had given five only to the Italians (Paolini, Olivieri, Caetani, Benvenuti and Sabbione).

I answered, repeating the agreed concept, according to which I had proposed two decorations for the two French officers who came out alive at the Beitang and two Japanese.

The French, besides two officers and Caetani, who oversaw the Italian detachment, were also decorating two civilians who had fought in the French Legation, contributing valiantly to the defense. I added that if the Ministry wanted to decorate all officers at the Siege then it was free to do so, and I was sending a list of them; furthermore, if they wanted to decorate all the personnel of the Legations, again they were free to do so. But in this case, I asked to exclude at least the people of the Russian corps *for the way they had behaved.*

On leaving Beijing I read on the newspapers that the Italian Government had decorated all the military and the members of the Russian Legation, not those of the other Legations. From a letter of Lady MacDonald, I came to know that all the other Governments had written a letter of thanks to them *except* the Italian one.

While in Rome, I mentioned these points to Prinetti, adding that the Government had been more generous than I had asked, and on this I had no say; but I was sorry that, wanting to decorate some diplomats, we had chosen the Russians, after I proposed to exclude them, and we had not written to Macdonald, while all the other Governments had done so.

Prinetti answered that they did follow my instructions to the letter, so I should not complain.

I told him what I had written but he insisted that my memory was faulty and the Ministry did what I had asked for: I could check with the office in charge of the Protocol and then I would realize that: "Before complaining I should check better what I was talking about."

The office of the Protocol confirmed that they did follow my instructions. Then I asked for the papers and the good Brofferio, on reading my telegram, realized their mistake. Things were exactly as I remembered, he was upset and agreed that they had decorated the Russian where I had proposed to exclude them, and they had forgotten to write to the MacDonalds.

Barilari felt even worse, because the lightning from Prinetti would strike him, as the man in charge of that office of the Protocol, and he begged me not to *cast a dark shadow* on him. I assured him that I would let him explain the matter to the Minister, but he should tell him that I had not made any mistake in my telegram. We agreed on that course of action.

Prinetti was not forgetting anything and he asked again about that matter and if I had done my research. I told him that Barilari would brief him on the subject. The next time I returned to the Ministry, Prinetti curtly told me: "I hope that next time you will think twice about what you say: you were proposing that the decorations be awarded to the Legation of Russia!"

I found it a bit too hard to swallow, and I asked if he had read the text of my telegram. Barillari entered his office giving me a bad look, and I told him: "I have said nothing to the Minister but asked him to read my telegram before accusing me."

The effect of his reading had disastrous effects on the office for the Protocol, whose employees, according to the Minister, should be dragged in front of him and then "he would have kicked them out of the building". He even specified the anatomical position where his kicks would be ministered.

Clearly, Barillari promised to find out the responsible employee… and then, giving out several sighs, he went back to his office.

Two days later the letter for the MacDonalds was drawn

up and delivered and a few months later I received the order of Saint Vladimir from Russia...

I came to know that a few days later, after furious scenes, it not being possible to withdraw the decorations given to the Russians, Prinetti demanded that the Russian representative should decorate all the people of the Italian Legation.

The End

Giuseppe Salvago Raggi as Governor of Eritrea.

Giuseppe Salvago Raggi's house at Campale (2014).

Bibliography

Barzini, Luigi *Nell'Estremo Oriente* Ed. Renzo Streglio, Turin, 1903.

Brandt, Nat *Massacre in Shansi* iUniverse, New York, 1999.

Brauzzi, Alfredo, *La Crociera del Marco Polo*, Rivista Marittima, Roma, 2006.

Bickers, Robert, *The Scramble for China*, Allen Lane, London, 2011.

Collis, Maurice, *Foreign Mud*, Faber, London, 1946.

Conger, Sarah Pike, *Letters from China*, Hodder and Stoughton, London, 1909.

Criveller, Gianni & Paratico, Angelo *Five Centuries of Italians in Hong Kong & Macau. 1513-2013* Dante Alighieri Society of Hong Kong, Hong Kong, 2013.

Fattore, Fabio, *Gli Italiani che Invasero la Cina*, Sugarco, Milan, 2008.

Fairbank, John King, *The Great Chinese Revolution 1800-1985*, Harper & Row, New York, 1986.

Fleming, Peter, *The Siege at Peking*, Rupert Hart-Davis, London, 1959.

Francioni, Andrea, *Il Trattato Italo-Cinese del 1866*, Working Papers Series, Edizioni Cantagalli, Siena, 2003.

Frey, General H., *Français et Alliés au Pé-tchili*, Paris, Librairie Hachette et Cie, Paris, 1904.

Hoe, Susanna, *Women at the Siege. Peking 1900*, The Women's History Press, Oxford, 2000.

Hooken, Mary, (Polly Condit Smith), *Behind the Scenes*, Columbia University Press, New York, 1911.

Hsu, Immanuel C.Y., *The Rise of Modern China*, Oxford University Press, Oxford, 2000.

Landor, Henry Savage *China and the Allies* 2 vols. Charles Scribner's Sons, New York, 1901.

Licata, Glauco *Notabili della Terza Italia* Edizioni Cinque Lune, Roma, 1968.

McAleavy, Henry, *The Chinese Woman*, George Allen & Unwin, London, 1959.

Marinelli, Maurizio and Andornino, Maurizio, *Italy's Encounters with Modern China*, Palgrave MacMillan, New York, 2014.

Moser, Michael & Moser Yeone, *Foreigners Within the Gates*, Oxford University Press, 1993.

Patrone, Stefano (a cura di) *L'Archivio Salvago Raggi. Registri contabili e filze di documenti. Gli Spinola di Ricchetta e Roccaforte.* Quaderni del Centro Studi e Documentazione di storia economica. Archivio Doria. Genoa, 2004.

Pichon, Stephen, *Dans La Bataille*, Méricant, Paris, 1908.

Rastelli, Achille, *Italiani a Shanghai*, Ugo Mursia Editore, Milan, 2011.

Salvago Raggi, Camilla *La nonna era bellissima* il Canneto, Genova, 2015. The pages of

Salvago Raggi, Camilla *L'ultimo sole sul prato* Longanesi, Milan 1982.

Salvago Raggi, Camilla *Di libro in libro la vita* Il Canneto, Genoa, 2015

Salvago Raggi, Giuseppe, *Lettere dall'Oriente*, Ecig, Genoa, 1992.

Salvago Raggi, Giuseppe, *Ambasciatore del Re. Memorie di un diplomatico dell'Italia liberale*, Le Lettere, Florence, 2011.

Seymour, Admiral Sir Edward, *My Naval Career and Travels*, Smith & Elder, London, 1911.

Smith, Shirley Ann, *Imperial Designs. Italians in China 1900-1947* Fairleigh Dickinson University Press, Madison, 2012

Tamagna Frank M., *Italy's Interests and Policies in the Far East*, Institute of Pacific relations, New York, 1941.

Thomson, Roger *Twilight of the Gods in the Chinese Countryside: Christians, Confucians, and the Modernizing State, 1861-1911*, in Daniel H. Bays, ed. *Christianity in China from the Eighteenth Century to the Present* Stanford, Stanford University Press, 1996.

Varè, Daniele, *The Last Empress* Doubleday, Doran & company, Inc. New York, 1936.

Villani, Giovanni, Villani Matteo, Villani Filippo *Cronica. I-IV.* Sanson Coen, Florence, 1845-46.

Vinci, Renata, *Chinese public sentiments about Italy during the Sanmen Bay affair in the pages of the Shenbao*, International Communication of Chinese Culture. *Emotions and Collective Imagery in the Transition to Modernity*, vol. 3, n. 1, March 2016, pp. 117-144.

Waldersee, Alfred, Count von, *A Field-Marshal's Memoirs*, Hutchison, London, 1924.

Wu Yang *The Flight of the Empress* George Allen & Unwin, London, 1937

Zanoni Volpicelli, Eugenio *The China-Japan War. Compiled from Japanese, Chinese, and Foreign Sources*, Sampson Low, Marston, 1896.

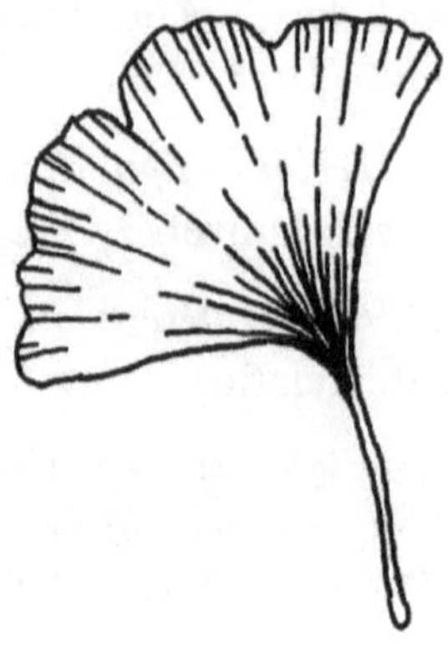

For more info visit the website::
www.gingkoedizioni.it
www.facebook/Gingkoedizioni

Gingko Edizioni
Vicoletto Valle, 2
37122 Verona
gingko@gingkoedizioni.it

National distribution CDA of Bologna

This book was printed by Gingko Edizioni
by Universal Book of Rende,
in the month of September 2019.

Stampato in Italia - Printed in Italy